DEFY THE IMMEDIATE
A JOURNEY OF FAILURE,
PERSEVERANCE, AND SUCCESS

DEFY THE IMMEDIATE

A Journey of Failure, Perseverance, and Success

———

By T.R. Shaw Jr.
Foreword by Dick Enberg

MISSION POINT PRESS

MISSION POINT PRESS

Published by Mission Point Press
2554 Chandler Rd.
Traverse City, MI 49686
(231) 421-9513
www.MissionPointPress.com

ISBN-13: 978-1-950659-24-1
Library of Congress Control Number:2019914301

Manufactured in the United States of America
First Edition/First Printing

TABLE OF CONTENTS

DEDICATION

To everyone who has gazed at the night sky and thought there must be more to life, that we are all here for a greater purpose.

To everyone who has served our great nation in uniform and stood in harm's way, defending our rights to dream big.

To my family, whose love and support have been critical to making me who I am today, especially my parents, Tom and Esther Shaw, and my wife, Kathy, who kept pushing me through my self-doubt, and my sister Elizabeth Shaw-Gescheidle, who has always been there and done more for our family than anyone will ever know.

Finally, to Will and Grace. Keep moving forward; the world awaits your greatness.

DISCLAIMER

———

The events depicted in this book are based on personal experiences from the author's memory. Names of some individuals have been omitted to protect the privacy of those involved.

ABOUT THE TITLE

It was May 1980. I was a sophomore at Central Michigan University, anxiously awaiting the commencement speaker, legendary sports broadcaster Dick Enberg, arguably CMU's most well-known alumnus.

Many of my friends and fraternity brothers were graduating – the Class of 1980 at the time was the largest in the history of the school – but I was mostly interested in Enberg.

Much of his address was about Dr. Charles Anspach, another legendary CMU figure who served as CMU president from 1939 to 1959. Anspach died in 1977, the year before I arrived on campus.

Anspach lifted the school from a small teachers' college to a major regional university. He was a true educator as well as an astute businessman and administrator who prepared CMU to be competitive well into the future. His foresight laid the groundwork for the coming generation of post-World War II baby boomers. Under his tenure, brick and mortar projects tripled the size and enrollment of the school. I spent many of my college hours in the journalism department and the Central Michigan LIFE newsroom on the lower level – we refused to call it the basement – of Anspach Hall.

Still, until Enberg's speech, I knew little about the man whose namesake building I labored inside. Turns out that Enberg ended up at CMU because Anspach had recruited him with a $100 scholarship offer after the college president delivered Enberg's high school commencement address in the early 1950s in Armada, Michigan.

It was among the many occasions Anspach took to talk in speeches, lectures and relaxed discussions with students, organizations and at conventions in Michigan and the Midwest.

As I listened raptly to Enberg, he recalled one of Anspach's favorite catchphrases: *"Defy the Immediate."* It means you should persevere through difficulties and stick to your goals and ideals to be successful in business, education and life.

FOREWORD

by Dick Enberg, CMU Class of 1957

———

My days at Central Michigan University were some of the most important and enjoyable of my entire life. CMU and the people who passed through the hallowed halls of our beloved alma mater have gone on to be some of the greatest benefactors of society, not just in Michigan and the Midwest, but around the world. Many fellow Chippewas have found solid success in sports, in the media, in education, in business, and in medicine.

T.R. Shaw has captured many familiar stories of college life, including the challenges and struggles in finding success. Life has a way of rewarding those who persevere and work hard. It's not always easy, but it is immensely rewarding. This I know to be true.

Although a generation apart, both Shaw and I started with a dream, which was nourished by great and giving CMU professors, as well as the many opportunities provided by a burgeoning campus. We both became involved with media at CMU, learned to love our university, even shared some time with the U.S. Navy. Shaw shares some poignant stories, not only from CMU, but life on active duty, where intense competition and difficult situations challenged him. He also shares stories of the funeral business, where he frequently had to deal with tragedy, emotions, difficult situations and a changing cultural landscape, including the death of his father and preserving a family business.

As a teenaged freshman, I was inspired by Dr. Charles Anspach, CMU president, who took the school from a small teachers' college to a major university, paving the way for a new generation of movers and shakers. His mantra of "Defy the Immediate" inspired me to tackle some of life's toughest and confusing moments, and gave me confidence to keep moving onward and upward.

In his motivational memoir, Shaw has captured the essence of his generation's convictions that much has been expected and much has been accomplished.

He will leave you with a powerful message that life can be very rewarding as long as we keep moving forward.

(Dick Enberg passed away unexpectedly just weeks after he wrote this. It may have been one of his last of many acts to help a fellow Chippewa. Although the author never met Enberg in person, they exchanged many emails, all upbeat and full of admiration for their alma mater. The author is grateful for Enberg's help and their shared enthusiasm and lifelong love for Central Michigan University.)

PREFACE

———

Leadership and success take many avenues. Some people seem to gravitate toward it. Others struggle endlessly in a futile attempt to achieve it.

My leadership journey began when I was young, took me to education, to the military, to the funeral business, and to community and professional leadership. My life experiences have made me a leader, but the journey was never easy. I will share personal stories of failure and success to help you on *your* journey. No single formula or template fits all leadership endeavors.

Military service is not an easy calling. It requires immense dedication, hard work, separation from family and loved ones, and it often results in frustration, loneliness, anxiety, doubt and fear. It often places you in harm's way few can comprehend and appreciate. Yet it can be one of the most rewarding things you can do with your life.

I entered the military because it was a high and noble calling and I wanted to make a difference in the world. I believe I have. My career, on active duty and in the reserve, had moments of mountaintop achievement when I swelled with pride and satisfaction, and valleys of deep despair where it took every shred of faith and every ounce of courage I could muster to keep going. Those challenging times form character and create leaders.

After active duty, I came home, returned to school, and took over my family funeral business. I had an amazing simultaneous career as a funeral director, business professional, community leader and Navy reservist.

My goal in writing this book is to inform, entertain, inspire, and – most of all – educate, or at least help, those who aim to become leaders. Whether it is in the military or in civilian life, the principles and techniques are the same.

One thing I learned as I slowly progressed through the ranks is that the most important trait of a leader is mentoring and leading the way for new generations of leaders.

We can take courses, examine models of success and emulate those we admire, or we can do what most people do and make original mistakes. I made many original mistakes and lived to talk about them. I overcame those missteps and was better for it.

If I can help others avoid the mistakes I made, then I've done my job. I hope you can identify with my stories and gain insight from them. You may laugh or cry and, hopefully, take away a few nuggets to use in your life's journey. Enjoy the ride!

CHAPTER 1

Humble Beginnings in a New Age
– Reaching for the Moon

"We set sail on this new sea because there is new knowledge to be gained, and new rights to be won, and they must be won and used for the progress of all people."

– John F. Kennedy, "Going to the Moon" speech,
Rice Stadium, Sept. 12, 1962

Like most kids growing up in the 1960s I watched the space race with utter fascination – from Kennedy's famous speech challenging us to go the moon before the decade was over, through Sputnik, the Mercury 7, Gemini, Apollo programs and the moon landing at Tranquility Base on July 20, 1969. I was a Space Age kid.

I read everything I could about rockets, space and the stars. I knew more about the astronauts than I did about any star athlete of the day. Like a lot of kids, I wanted to *be* an astronaut. Heck, I even had the G.I. Joe with a silver spacesuit and Mercury capsule.

As a child, anything seemed possible. I remember well the day of the moon landing. I was nine and attending summer camp. The counselors brought us all into the recreation hall and we sat on the floor cross-legged, watching a small black-and-white television propped up on a chair.

The counselors adjusted the rabbit ear antenna until the fuzzy picture became reasonably sharp. TV tuning is a lost art today.

We watched as CBS anchorman Walter Cronkite, as familiar a face as anyone in that era, described Neil Armstrong stepping off the lunar module and announcing:

"That's one small step for a man. One giant leap for Mankind."

At that time most of us kids watched in awe, but we couldn't grasp how significant an event that really was. The adults, including Cronkite, wept as we witnessed what was arguably one of man's most spectacular achievements.

For me and my buddies, the moon landing was expected. We grew up in a time of high expectations and going to the moon was a logical progression of something we set out to do as a nation. We baby boomers are a generation that grew up in brief post-war peace. Vietnam was heating up, and the world was dramatically changing, but the 1960s from my perspective were a time to dream and look to the future.

Man's voyage to the moon set the standard for what I felt was expected from my generation. We were to grow up with unlimited possibilities. The world was our oyster. After the moon landing, the world was a smaller place.

My grandmother spent a small fortune taking me to the hobby shop to buy model rockets, solid fuel engines and rocketry supplies. It was the hobby of choice in those days, and the names Centuri, Estes, Payloader II, and Laser X still bring back warm memories. I firmly believe that one my three-stagers is now passing Saturn. The sulfuric smell of a burnt solid fuel engine was a fragrance to behold.

As we grew older, we began realizing that the world was more complicated and harsher than those carefree days. The Vietnam War was raging and coming into our living rooms every night. I had a cousin who worried he would be drafted. War protesters, sit-ins, hippies and draft dodging left us confused.

As we moved into high school and learned more about the world, we began to realize that democracy, freedom, government and patriotism meant different things to different people. We not only discovered diversity of opinion and idealism but also learned that the world was bigger and less stable than we thought. We had to look into ourselves to examine what it all meant to us. What world would we face in the next 50 years?

By the time I was in high school in the mid-'70s, the nation was in deep recession. The excitement of the moon landing had faded and an energy crisis was upon us. The space program had gone into hibernation and we seemed to lack the will as a nation to improve things. I remember long lines at gas stations and worry about the future. All our optimism as starry-eyed youths seemed sadly utopian. I figured this must be what happens when you grow up. Things in life will never get easier. A fatalistic attitude began to take root.

I was fortunate to have parents, family and friends who drilled into my sister and I the importance of college. Over and over I was told I would need a college education to succeed in life. As I looked around at the world in those days, it was clear that without education, there would be no future for me. In my hometown, Battle Creek, cereal giant Kellogg wasn't hiring.

It was a scary time, I wasn't a good student academically, and I worried about getting into college, let alone graduating someday. It seemed overwhelming.

Once again, I was fortunate. I attended schools where teachers were leaders. Several outstanding educators pushed me toward my potential.

One of the most memorable was Joe Brigante, my junior high school civics teacher, who on his own for many years organized a three-day field trip to Washington, D.C. He sought grants to subsidize it and drafted other teachers and parents as chaperones. He didn't have to do this, but it was part of his character and part of his professional duty as an educator.

My 8th grade trip, my first visit to our Capitol, was and remains today my most memorable. I've been in Washington many, many times, but that first trip led by Mr. Brigante cannot be equaled as a life-changing event. It opened my eyes to the grandeur of our nation and the privilege of democracy and freedom. We saw the special places and important documents that help define our nation. It was incredible.

Sure, we were kids and goofed off a lot. For many of us it was our first time on an airplane and our first time away from home. One night several of us in our room at the Crystal City Marriott lit cigars and played poker. We acted like big shots and ended up having a cloud of smoke roll down the hall. Mr. Brigante came in, broke up the party and doused the cigars. He never really chastised us. We expected some repercussion, but it never came. We thought we were in deep trouble, but no further mention was made of the episode. He probably thought it was hilarious.

Later when touring Arlington National Cemetery, knowing I was the son of a funeral director and lived in a funeral home, he shouted *"Hey, Shaw, I bet you are really digging this place aren't you?"* Everyone laughed; it broke the tension because most of us didn't really know how to act in a cemetery.

Years later a Navy trip took me back to Washington to attend a class at the National Defense University at Fort McNair. I was sitting in my hotel room, studying and enjoying a quiet evening, when I observed a bus full of kids pull up. They unloaded and in moments the serenity was shattered by 50 or so kids running and screaming in the hallways. When I took a study break, I discovered that they had already drained the pop machines.

At first I was upset, but as I thought more about it, that's exactly what we had done 30 years earlier, though I think we were more respectful! Anyway, my angst disappeared when I thought back to my first Washington visit and remembered Mr. Brigante.

I thanked God there were still people with the drive to take a group of kids to Washington and put up with them. Who knows how many of them might be inspired to public service because of it. Perhaps there was a future congressman, senator or commander-in-chief among them. I shed a few tears thinking about that first trip to D.C. and where I had come since.

Joe Brigante was an outstanding and popular teacher. The U.S. Jaycees once recognized him as one of "Ten Outstanding Young People." He struggled with obesity when I was in junior high though over the course of a year and beyond dropped a tremendous amount of weight. When I was in college, I was saddened to learn that he had died of a massive heart attack. We lost a great teacher and friend.

In high school, I was again blessed with one of those rare teachers who do much more than teach. Peter Ives at Battle Creek Central High School was one of the people most responsible for setting my bearings in life and making me see my potential.

He taught biology, but more important he taught life skills through his own experiences. Some days he would just talk about life and things that had happened to him.

He wouldn't tolerate distractions in class. Other teachers considered him an egotist but, as I've come to realize, most true leaders have a healthy ego. An ego is a healthy thing as long as it is kept in check and used for good. The world is full of egomaniacs who have no sense of responsibility. Narcissistic, pompous pride serves no one and examples abound today.

Ives was the first person who taught us pneumonic memory devices. The one I remember most was based on his earlier life in Gary, Indiana, which he talked about too often. It was the order of taxonomy, the scientific classification of *Kingdom, Phylum, Class, Order, Family, Genus, and Specie.* His device to remember the groups was *"King Peter Comes over from Gary Saturday."* He said he came up with it when he was dating his wife. These pneumonic devices were a great help in my later schooling and especially in the Navy learning systems, navigation and engineering.

Ives was demanding and many students couldn't cut it in his classroom. Those who tried hard and met the challenges were rewarded and praised, but it wasn't easy. He convinced us that there was no place for second best and trying was more important than doing. Because he clearly set the bar of what was expected, I worked harder in his classroom than any other. I learned not only biology, but much about science and how things work, including our own minds. I learned how to get organized. I discovered that child-like potential still inside me, but it needed to be cultivated and directed.

Naturally, the good students gravitated to his classroom and he had the respect of those who met his challenges. He deserved any awards he received, but I'm sure his biggest reward is knowing he developed people who eventually made a difference in the world. I am proud to be an Ives' alumnus.

Another memorable teacher was John Rasmussen, who taught literature and "Western Thought." The title "Western Thought" made literature much more appealing and cooler – he was passionate about getting us to read the great classics of our time. Mr. Rasmussen was a graduate of the University of Iowa and an avid Hawkeye, the only one I ever really knew. He was very youthful looking and to this day shows little sign of aging.

Once he assigned us to read a classic novel, the name of which I don't recall. In fact, I just skimmed it. When he gave a test on the book, one of the questions was about the main character, Ryeworth. I had no clue who, or what he was about, so I made up a response. I said "Ryeworth" is a bartering term heard around the English marketplace on many occasions: "Say old chap, what's Rye Worth today?" Needless to say, he flunked me on the test, but commented that he loved the creativity! I got a little more serious after that and ended up doing well in his class and took several other classes he offered. He was an inspiring teacher.

I set my sights on a lofty goal for my life. Before I discovered journalism, I had decided to be a dentist and I started working toward that goal. The problem was, it was a brutally competitive profession and I just didn't have the grades to get into a decent college that in turn would get me into dental school. I talked with my own dentist and realized that maybe that goal wasn't achievable and I probably didn't have the aptitude or dexterity for it anyway.

It was during this time I first considered the military as a career. I thought I could enlist and become a Navy dental technician and then get to college and dental school through the military. It was about that time the ASVAB (Armed Services Vocational Aptitude Battery) was being given at my school. The ASVAB is a test that helps students set goals and is a great asset to military recruiters. I thought if I could do well on the ASVAB, I might consider joining the Navy as an enlisted dental technician (DT) and possibly progress up to Navy dentist.

A few weeks after the test, the results came back and I went over them with a Marine recruiter. He said the scores suggested I should be an engineer. I was flabbergasted. I couldn't possibly be an engineer, I hated math. I told him I wanted to be a dentist and he acted quite surprised. I told him I had thought about becoming a Navy DT, but he knew little about that field and couldn't give me much advice.

My first contact with the military as a high school student was not good, but it did reinforce the importance of college. I thought the military could wait and I later talked with family friends who encouraged me to get my college degree first and then enlist in the military as an officer if I was still interested.

That was the best advice I ever received. That's exactly what I did.

After that, college became my priority, but I still didn't know what I wanted to be.

Fortunately, I fell into another area of study that fascinated me. I started working on the school newspaper and yearbook. I started writing in junior high school for the newspaper. It was a big kick to see my byline. I never thought of writing as more than something fun to get your name in print, but I ended up being both a writer and photographer for the junior and high school paper and yearbook. I used the camera to get myself into everything at school. I became known as the yearbook photographer and people flocked to me. It was a great social tool, but at the time it was just a hobby.

For many years my dad, a University of Michigan alumnus, and several of his friends organized the local Michigan Golf Outing in Battle Creek, which featured ALL the Michigan coaches. Bo Schembechler, Johnny Orr, Bill Frieder, Don Canham and most of the assistants came, played golf and spoke at a dinner event at the Battle Creek Country Club.

In those days it was strictly a stag (men only) event and one they all looked forward to. The athletic staff was pretty much autonomous of the school and did as they pleased. The coaches joked at the dinner and said things that no HR department would allow today. Orr, the basketball coach, had us rolling hysterically on the floor. He said things that would make a sailor blush. In fact, that's what ended it. Political correctness was taking root. Eventually, U-M started managing these events and hand-picking who represented the school and training them on what was appropriate. I remember attending the dinner for many years and they eventually became somewhat boring.

But that first year, I spent the day riding around in a golf cart, taking pictures and interviewing coaches. I put together an article and it became my first true work of journalism. I submitted it to the local weekly shopper and a week later I had a full page spread with my story and photos – and my byline! I was hooked.

High school is a time of growth and I tried hard to be involved in everything I could.

I wanted to play football, but Battle Creek Central was a big school and I was too small. The competition for the team was strong, and I was too slow to be a running back or receiver and too small to be a lineman or defensive back. I had played in junior high school as a center, but was killed every time the ball was snapped because I couldn't look up fast enough. I did become the long-snapper for punts and kicks.

I didn't have a burning desire to compete for a spot on the gridiron and figured I could do other things. In hindsight, I wish I had had the courage to try. I missed the camaraderie, pride and satisfaction that come with being a football player, especially when we won big games. There were many times I sat in the stands Friday night regretting I wasn't on the field.

But I did join the swim team. Although I never really amounted to much, we did have a lot of fun. We had superstars on the team those years, including Mark Lancaster, who was one of my best friends growing up and competed in the state championship. A few of his records still stand today in area pools. He became a star swimmer at Michigan State University and competed in the Big Ten. He had a body similar to Michael Phelps. We were blessed to have a great coach in Larry Wegener, who was an All-American Swimmer at CMU a few years earlier. He reluctantly became a coach, but grew into the job and ended up becoming a great friend. He brought innovation and drive back to the swimming program at Battle Creek Central and eventually became the school's athletic director.

We were lucky to be able to train in the old Battle Creek Central Fieldhouse, which used to be the recreational building that was part of Dr. John Harvey Kellogg's adjacent Sanitarium. The building was sold to Battle Creek Public Schools for a dollar after the depression and demise of the institution. The Fieldhouse still serves as the school's basketball arena.

Back in the Sanitarium days, the pool was divided into a men's and women's side; there was no co-ed swimming. The school took out the bulkhead dividing it and created one big pool that was shallow in the middle and deep on both ends. We had a strategic advantage by training in a 40-yard pool and swimming longer lengths. Coach Wegener had us train early in the morning and in the afternoon, so we did a lot of laps. He creatively got the school to have a first hour aquatics class as a physical education credit. You could enroll in it as many times as you wished. So, we came in at 7 a.m., trained hard for an hour and at 8 a.m. other students, mostly girls, came in and we had a pool party a few times a week! I just remember it being a great way to start the day.

I was lucky when I got to swim one leg of a relay in a meet. When superstars surround you, it's easy to tell yourself you're not that good. Trouble is you begin to believe it and it becomes a self-fulfilling prophecy. Sometimes you might not be the lead goose in the flock, but as long as you are in the flock, you can hang with them.

The only real advantage I gained in my years of swimming came later when I attended Navy Officer Candidate School. I was the only person in my company who could decently swim the butterfly. I wasn't good, but I could at least go 50 yards without being disqualified. So my contribution to sports day was swimming the butterfly, which was pretty pathetic.

All the President's Men; The Dawn of the Information Age

In 1974 a national crisis known as Watergate gripped the nation. It culminated in August when President Richard M. Nixon became the nation's first president to resign, making Michigan's own longtime congressman Gerald R. Ford the new president. I remember the earlier night of the Battle Creek Central-Lakeview football game when the announcer told the crowd that Nixon had nominated Ford as his choice to replace Spiro Agnew as vice president, following Agnew's resignation. It was a time of great chaos for our nation, but it brought journalism to the forefront, especially that of two Washington Post reporters, Bob Woodward and Carl Bernstein.

Watergate elevated the profession of reporter and journalist and ushered in the information age. The movie "All the President's Men" told the Watergate story. Actors Robert Redford and Dustin Hoffman played the roles of Woodward and Bernstein. I became fascinated with the press and wanted to get more involved in reporting and publishing.

I became co-editor of the PAEAN, our high school yearbook. I probably spent too much time working on the publications, but it was a refuge from the social traumas of high school. We learned to crop photos, use grease pencils, and write captions. I eventually knew everyone in school from identifying photos. I learned how to process black-and-white photos and other darkroom skills.

We considered ourselves lucky when the Blizzard of 1978 shut down classes for two weeks and our adviser, Bonnie Brown, let us in the school. The staff worked on the yearbook without the interruption of pesky classes every 55 minutes.

The day the yearbooks arrived at the end of my senior year was one of the most euphoric of my life. I took great pride in what we had produced in our months of hard teamwork; it was a labor of love for a small group of friends.

My first venture into opinion writing came when I started a column, "Shaw's Scene," in our school newspaper. A scathing column about the student courtyard, which was just outside the publications room, provoked an unexpected response from the principal. The courtyard was a gathering place for students we referred to as "burnouts." They smoked, were out of the mainstream and were ones we assumed weren't going anywhere in life. Yes, we engaged in a little class warfare back then.

The column referred to them as "slobs" because they left cigarette butts all over the courtyard. I suggested that the school clean up the mess.

The principal, Lou Martin, took offense that I called the students who inhabited the courtyard "slobs." This was my first encounter with First Amendment rights and freedom of the press, as limited as it was.

It was unsettling knowing I stirred up trouble but Mrs. Brown stood by me as the principal chastised me. It was a tremendous learning experience. I enjoyed the power of the press, but also learned that with that power comes responsibility.

The most rewarding thing about the entire episode was that the courtyard *was* cleaned up and within a week there were concrete urns in place for the cigarette butts. It was a remarkable feeling, knowing I affected change with something I had written. Mrs. Brown praised me. It lit a fire and I knew what I wanted to use my college studies to pursue a career in journalism.

A Titan Among Us

In my hometown we were blessed to have a quality newspaper, the Battle Creek Enquirer, operated by three generations of benevolent publishers. Albert L. Miller bought the paper early in the 20th Century; it was later run by his son Robert B. Miller and then his grandson, Bob Miller Jr.

The Millers ran the newspaper during the glory years of Battle Creek and were close to the local titans of industry, including those of the Kellogg and Post dynasties. The Millers were as powerful as any of the cereal barons. C.W. Post brought the senior Miller to Battle Creek from his home state of Kansas around the turn of the century.

Bob Jr. grew up with my father and was one of his closest friends. Before he returned to Battle Creek, Bob Jr. was the publisher of the *Idaho Statesman* in Boise. His son Greg was my age and we became close during his summer visits to Battle Creek. Greg's grandfather, Bob Sr., or "Big Bob," as we called him, had a beautiful country estate home on the Minges Brook where Greg stayed when he came to visit. He stayed in The Lodge, as it was called. It was built on the brook and is a miniature version of the main house on the property. Bob and his first wife Jean built The Lodge and lived in it while the main house was being built in the 1940s. The Lodge was the site of great parties, some of which Big Bob knew about and some he didn't. It was at this time I got to know Big Bob well and learned about the publishing business. We had many conversations around his fieldstone fireplace and it made me even more excited about getting into journalism. The home is now the headquarters of the Miller Foundation.

Big Bob had enormous wealth, but he was humble and down-to-earth. But being around him gave me a sense of affluence and what could be possible if you worked hard.

Greg and I cruised around in the summers in Big Bob's red Mercedes 280 SL convertible, which he let us drive. He called it the Lady Bug. If we were lucky, he gave us a ride in his Bentley, which he brought out on rare occasions.

When he traveled, Big Bob always went first class and was a frequent visitor to Europe. I loved to talk to him about the fabulous places he had been. He was an awesome storyteller. He did many things for Battle Creek and numerous buildings bear his name. Robert B. Miller was one of the most significant people to live in Battle Creek who wasn't connected to cereal.

He was instrumental in many brick and mortar projects in Battle Creek and was especially generous with Kellogg Community College, which he helped build. In the spring of 2003, the college established the Miller College, which offered a baccalaureate degree, as a Robert B. Miller legacy. It allowed students to get a four-year degree close to home, a first for a Michigan community college.

But the financial realities of a public-private partnership nearly drained the Miller Foundation and the college closed after a few years. The remaining students were enrolled into Western Michigan University.

Still solvent and dynamic, the Miller Foundation continues to play a huge role in civic affairs.

Big Bob's wealth came from owning many newspapers. At one time he owned Federated Publications, which had several newspapers in Michigan. When he retired he sold the chain to the Gannett Corp. and Bob Jr. returned home to become publisher of the Enquirer.

Bob Jr. had already been associated with Gannett and was close to Gannett chairman Al Neuharth, a titan in the newspaper business. Neuharth founded USA Today and took Gannett into the information age. He was a transformative figure in the newspaper business and Bob talked of him frequently. He shared memos with me about what Neuharth expected when he visited one of the corporation's newspapers. I never met Neuharth, but knew of him vicariously through the Millers. I followed with great interest the development of USA Today and bought stock in Gannett and followed the company's fortunes.

I got even more hooked on journalism because of those relationships and knew more firmly that newspapering was for me.

Lesson Learned

Never underestimate the power of dreams. When we were young we dreamed big because we didn't have the perspective to dream small. We weren't tainted with negativity, a learned fault. There is value in remembering the dreams of your youth when you were likely unencumbered with big problems or uncertainty.

Somewhere along the way, we dismissed the big dreams we had when life became more complicated.

If you are at a certain age in life, it would be beneficial to reconnect with your "inner child" and remember those grandiose dreams you once had. What kept you from pursuing them? Was it fear, time, money, opportunity?

If you could go back and do it all over, how would you do it differently? We can learn from those dreams and rekindle them. If not, we can rekindle enthusiasm and childlike energy and apply them to today's dreams and aspirations.

Find the childlike energy and adolescent curiosity that knew no limitations, apply it and use it to Defy the Immediate in today's problems.

CHAPTER 2

Down on the Farm

"We eat every day, and if we do it in a way that doesn't recognize value, it's contributing to the destruction of our culture and of agriculture. But if it's done with a focus and care, it can be a wonderful thing. It changes the quality of your life."

— Alice Waters

If there was one great aspect of growing up in the Sixties, it was the opportunity to experience the vanishing agrarian work ethic. In an age where many kids don't know where milk comes from, I was lucky to have spent part of my childhood around agriculture.

My grandparents, Wayne and Lillie Smith, were among Michigan's best apple growers. They operated three orchards in Athens, about 15 miles south of Battle Creek. My mother, Esther, was a farm girl and she made sure my sister, Elizabeth, and I experienced farm life.

I spent many weekends in Athens and in the orchards during all seasons. I saw firsthand the work that goes into preparing, growing and harvesting apples. I watched my grandfather work long and hard doing manual labor and equally long hours tinkering with his machines with his close friend and mechanical genius, Roscoe Landfair.

Weeks were spent each spring pruning trees to maximize the crop; Wayne was an expert in what to prune and what not to prune. He taught dozens of workers how to meticulously trim the trees.

By summer there was a huge pile of cut sprouts, which sometimes reached 15 feet. They had now dried and were ready for the annual bonfire in the middle of the orchard. In almost a ritual, the sprouts were burned as darkness fell and we roasted hot dogs and marshmallows over crackling flames.

Part of one of the orchards was a 40-acre dense woods with dozens of walnut trees. When my grandfather was very young, he and his father planted many of the trees, which were to be harvested in his old age to fund his retirement. They

The author shows off a ripe apple alongside orchard manager Bill Landfair on the farm of his grandparents, Wayne and Lillie Smith. In the background is the modified Allis Chalmers tractor with the reverse chassis and added forklift.

grew to epic size and in his last years the farm was harvested. This insurance plan was better than anything the government could provide.

The woods were a wonderland of nature's beauty. Spring was the best season as morel mushrooms sprouted everywhere and wildflowers such as Dutchman's breeches, jack-in-the-pulpits, and dozens of others thrived. Grandma knew every flower. She was remarkable.

Once, while with a friend, we stumbled across the mother lode of morels under an apple tree. We pulled out our shirttails and filled each other's shirts. Everyone was excited when we came up to the house. Grandma cleaned and fried them up. I've never had anything so tasty!

Frequently, we were dispatched with a list to the local village store, Henkel's Market, to pick up mealtime staples. My grandparents had an open account that we often took advantage of, picking up some sweet treats not on the list. The three-block walk "uptown" usually included a stop at the post office where they still had a postal box for their mail, and maybe a diversion to the local soda fountain for a cherry phosphate. Small-town life was wonderful!

The farmhouse in Athens was a beehive of activity and Wayne and Lillie not only ran the farm and sales business, but they raised a second generation.

My mom's older sister Leila married young and lost her husband, Charles Osgood, in a plane crash. Leila and her two children, Bob and Marilyn, returned to the farmhouse and became part of a multi-generational household.

Leila and the children all worked in the apple business growing up. Wayne and Lillie, for all intents and purpose, raised them as their own children. Although the orchards are long gone, Bob and his wife, Donna, still live in the family farmhouse. As cousins, we had a great time on the farm.

Lunchtime, or dinner as they called it, was the biggest meal of the day and all the women helped prepare it. We ate like kings. Apples, meat and potatoes were always part of the meal. In today's health-conscious society, it is difficult to look back on all the food we ate, but those working in the field had to eat big to get the energy needed to finish the work. My grandpa was always lean, strong and healthy, and he lived to 86. He spent his days outdoors, walking and working, and ate lots of food.

My grandpa was one of the community's largest employers. Beyond the family, he had two full-time managers, Ed (Buster) Cheyne and Bill Landfair, who worked for him most of their lives and managed much of the operations. For the harvest he hired several migrant workers to pick the apples. He called them the "Southern Boys." They came up from southern states in late summer and stayed into the fall. They were all white Americans and mostly poor. Hispanic workers were just coming on the scene in those days.

He built a couple of well-equipped and comfortable bunkhouses in the orchard and always made sure they were well taken care of. He loaned them shotguns and let them hunt after hours. He had many loyal employees who returned year after year because he was a good boss. He was fair but very demanding. He pounded into the pickers the ethic of treating apples like eggs. Bruised apples don't sell and he was meticulous in how he trained people. He wouldn't tolerate sloppy picking and bad apples.

Here's a sort of a strange sidebar to the Southern Boys. As a child I hung out and talked with many of them while they worked. They told tall tales and funny stories. Most of them were not well-educated and spoke with a drawl foreign to our part of the world.

My next encounter with southerners would be in the Navy. For the longest time I had a real mental block that someone with that drawl is *not* ignorant or uneducated, even as I worked with well-educated and articulate officers and enlisted men from southern states. On the flip side of that after being away from Michigan for a long time, I was amazed how well I could understand everyone and that we actually had our own accent and dialect. Who knew?

The seasonal cycle started early in the spring when the orchards were cleaned up and the winter's damage assessed. Then, around May, the apple blossoms burst forth in one of nature's most spectacular displays of white and pink flowers. We often had picnics in the orchards and once even had a family reunion on a beautiful spring day during apple blossom time. Grandpa would put a pallet on his forklift and we would all sit on it. He would lift it up above the treetops, about 15 feet, and drive around the orchard with all of us at tree-top level. It was a great experience, a little scary, and – in hindsight – extremely dangerous. OSHA didn't exist then.

Apple blossom time also meant contracting with beekeepers to pollinate the blossoms. It was always a struggle getting the weather and availability of bees to coincide. Few people realize how important this detail is to produce a fruit crop.

Grandpa was a mechanical genius; you could frequently find him and Roscoe tinkering with tractors and equipment. He often bartered for old equipment and fixed it to use in the orchard. Hardly any machine he owned did what it was originally built for.

The most interesting piece of machinery was his combination forklift/trac-tor. He took an old Allis-Chalmers tractor and turned the seat, chassis and transmission around and mounted an old Clark Equipment forklift between the large wheels. He had to counterbalance it with huge weights on the other end. He always drew attention when he drove the tractor down the road "back-ward," but the forklift was extremely useful in the barns and loading trucks because he had three-way lifting capability and could hoist a pallet of apple crates and move it forward and sideways.

I continually asked when I could drive the tractor and his stock answer was always "Tuesday." Tuesday never came.

He also had a grading and polishing machine in the barn that had a conveyor chain with openings of various sizes. Fresh picked apples were loaded at one end of the conveyor and, as they went down, they were polished and the bigger apples stayed on and the smaller ones fell through. Thus, all the apples were graded by size, quality, and variety. It was a fascinating process to watch. Lillie's sister, Ura, frequently helped at harvest time and was a valuable asset in the barn.

Grandpa grew 32 varieties of apples and a few varieties of pears. Fall harvest was a special time when apples and cider were sold in the home barn market. People came from near and far to buy his apples.

About two-thirds of his crop was sold commercially. At one time he was an apple supplier to Gerber Baby Foods in Fremont, Michigan. He was always proud of that relationship and we still think of Grandpa's apples when we see Gerber products. Many trips were also made to Eastern Market in Detroit and to a market in Toledo.

Lillie was in charge of the retail sales in the barn on fall weekends and had a gentle but iron fist. She had her own genius when it came to setting up displays and marketing. The sales barn was always clean and decorated for Halloween and Thanksgiving and apple displays were set up to promote the apples being harvested at that time. It was immaculate and creative. I learned a lot about service and presentation from Lillie. They operated on strictly a cash basis, using a fishing tackle box to keep money in and make change.

I have to laugh when I go to the store these days and see apples graded as "fancy." Lillie would select fancies to display and they generally were the size of large grapefruits or softballs, nothing like the smaller standard today.

Lillie had a great relationship with the local Native American tribe, the Nottawaseppi Huron Band of Potawatomi, who were placed in a corner of Calhoun County in 1820 after they ceded much of their ancestral lands in the area as Michigan became a state.

The 20th Century wasn't very good to the tribe. In the 1960s the members still lived fairly primitively on the reservation southwest of the village, but they always had a symbiotic relationship with the village and its citizens. My grandfather hired many tribal members to help on the farm. Many found work during the fall harvest in the Smith Orchards.

The tribe's biggest enterprise in those days was farming as well as craftwork and basket weaving that sustained them through sales or bartering. They were exceptionally good at crafting baskets in all shapes and sizes and sold them throughout the area. Today, they would be highly sought after and bring a hefty price. Lillie frequently worked with the tribe helping them sell baskets and craftwork. Often she would load Indian-made baskets with apples and sell them together. She became one of their biggest supporters and distributors.

When I was born, the chief of the tribe brought my mother a beautiful basket as a gift, which she often used to cart me around.

In 1995, the tribe gained official federal recognition as a nation, which they'd sought for more than 50 years. This entitled the membership to a sovereign government and paved the way for new enterprises; the tribe ultimately started the FireKeepers Casino in Battle Creek. The tribe has risen well above the poverty that plagued its members throughout its history. FireKeepers is now one of the largest employers in the area and one of the largest gaming and entertainment venues in the Midwest. The reservation, although still isolated, has seen tremendous growth as the tribe stretches its economic muscle in southwest Michigan.

The casino earnings have allowed the tribe to do many things. The tribal police department is the main police agency on the reservation, the Athens village and the township. The tribe also has set up a revenue sharing plan with the county and several townships, which gives back millions of dollars annually. The tribe's newfound wealth has made it a partner with NASCAR as it is now the title sponsor of the FireKeepers 400 at the Michigan International

After the author's grandfather, Wayne Smith, retired as a fruit farmer, he lived with the Shaw family. The author is wearing his classic "rockin' the '70s" outfit and enjoying the scene with his grandpa at the Detroit Auto Show.

Speedway, one of the two major races each year. The members have come a long way since their official recognition and my childhood.

Back to Grandpa Wayne. I also had the opportunity to go with him to the cider mill and help make cider; what a treat that was! I remember sitting in line at the press behind an Amish farmer with a horse-drawn wagon with a load of apples. Many growers brought their apples to the cider mill. It was a cooperative effort; no one had their own press because it wasn't economical.

Most of the apples for cider were "drops." When apples got too ripe on the tree they fell and were too ripe to sell for anything but cider. Also, the apples that were too small to sell went into the cider bin. To make good cider, Wayne and Lillie mixed tart and sweet apples for a better tasting blend. Both my grandparents were excellent cider brewmasters and took care in making a quality product.

After the apples were pressed, the cider was poured into wooden barrels and brought back to the barn market. Customers came with glass jugs and we tapped the barrels with wooden spigots. It wasn't until later that they started putting the cider in plastic gallon jugs, something Lillie didn't care for. The last fall they were in operation before they retired, they sold a gallon of cider for 96 cents. With the 4 percent sales tax, it was $1.00 per gallon, easy math. What a deal!

Wayne also had a special barrel of cider we weren't supposed to know about. He kept it behind the barn and let it ferment. When the weather got below freezing, the water separated from the alcohol. He had a private stash of "Apple Jack" and only shared it with a few close buddies!

Lillie died on Thanksgiving Day 1974 and that pretty much put an end to the Smith Orchards and Farm Market. Without her, Wayne didn't have the desire to continue. He tried for one year, but it wasn't the same and an era came to an end in 1975. Unfortunately, many other family operations have gone the same way as high-tech farming and agri-business have driven the simple family businesses out of existence.

I frequently visit other farm markets and cider mills in the fall, and it brings back fond memories of a simpler time. How I had wished they had kept the operation going. If I would have been a little older I would have loved to run the sales and marketing of a small farm market, but I doubt I could have ever done it as well or as successfully as my grandparents. They were from the generation that came through the Great Depression and were completely self-reliant. In their days they didn't have government regulations that stifle so many small businesses today.

What Wayne and Lillie can teach us today is priceless. They believed in the cycles of life, the rhythms of the earth. They were self-reliant and knew that hard work was the only way to success. They lived through the Great Depression and spring freezes that destroyed crops. They raised two generations and knew what it was like to survive lean times.

They made sure none of us would ever be without. They told stories of Depression-era life when they had little except faith; they didn't want for food because they grew their own. They were frugal, yet generous, and had great faith in their fellow human beings. They had an unwritten code of always helping others because they knew that they, too, could need help someday. They lived in a social society where everyone was taken at face value. They met obstacles with optimism and singleness of purpose. They expected the best of others and were always thankful for what they had.

They faced many hardships in their lifetimes and were the better for it. In their later years, they took time off in winters and spent weeks in Florida after everything was put away for the season.

A lot has been said about their generation, but that simple, humble, hard-working attitude is what our current society often lacks. We must never lose sight of those times. Wayne and Lillie Smith **Defied the Immediate** their entire life and gave two generations memories and experiences that can never be duplicated.

I'm eternally grateful I had a chance to experience a small part of it. I wish the kids growing up today could, too.

Lesson Learned

In today's fast-paced world, we often forget the value of agriculture and the profound impact it has on us. The convenience of picking up a gallon of milk on the way home is something we take for granted. We forget there is an industry of farmers, scientists and engineers who constantly find quicker, easier and better ways to get food from farm to table.

My grandparents lived in a time of self-sufficiency and self-reliance where the next crop, or next year's income, was never certain. Often they did without. Yet they always made do and shared what they had with others. There is much to be learned from the depression era generation. Most of us today have never experienced a food shortage or crop failure. I hope we never do.

But as our population expands it's unconscionable that anyone should go hungry. America is too abundant and too resourceful for anyone to face starvation and poverty, yet many children and seniors do, as hunger is commonplace in many parts of our nation and food banks struggle to keep up with demand.

We must not forget the importance of agriculture in our economic equation. If anyone can **Defy the Immediate** it's the American Farmer who faces drought, floods, insect plagues, frosts, market fluctuations and, yes, excessive government regulation. Where would our nation be without the farmer?

CHAPTER 3

___

Becoming an Urban Dweller

"We must all obey the great law of change. It is the most powerful law of nature."
— Sir Edmund Burke

When I was very young, we lived in a great suburban neighborhood, the Lakeview area of Battle Creek. It's the neighborhood I moved back to as an adult when I returned from the Navy and began my career in the funeral business.

My sister Elizabeth and I played with friends nearby and lived a carefree life, riding our bikes around quiet streets.

When I was about to enter fifth grade, my parents sat us down for a serious conversation. They had decided to remodel the apartment at our funeral home downtown and move the family there. My grandfather, Frank Shaw Jr., had bought the historic building in 1949 and converted it into a funeral home. The street was one of the most fashionable in town at the height of the industrial revolution early in the 20th Century. Originally called Maple Street, the industrial barons in Battle Creek made it Mansion Row. Ours was built by industrialist H.B. Sherman, who manufactured lawn sprinklers, mostly made from brass. It was a beautiful home.

We didn't want to leave our friends behind, but the offer that sealed the deal was the fact that we also acquired the family property on nearby Gull Lake. We would live in the apartment above the funeral home during the school year and spend summers at Gull Lake, about 17 miles from Battle Creek. We agreed and became students in the Battle Creek Public School system.

I started fifth grade and my sister was in second grade at Fremont Elementary, one of the oldest and most prestigious elementary schools in the city. We tried to stay close to our old friends, but when you aren't regularly engaged with them, you lose track. But we fit in easily in our new neighborhood, even while keeping many of our Lakeview friends.

Living in the small, third-floor funeral home apartment was a challenge. We made the best of it though, for 17 years. I can't tell you how many times my dad chewed me out for noisily running up and down the steps. "Be quiet!" were words that rang in my head.

One great thing about living there was that when Mom and Dad worked late, they could come upstairs for a bite and go back to work. They saved a lot of money living at the office and because we were only three blocks from downtown, there were many things to do afternoons, evenings and weekends.

Because of visitations and funerals, we also frequently went to dinner downtown. Our usual destination was Shrank's Cafeteria, where we could get in and get out quickly. This became our family dinner destination about three nights a week, leaving us great memories of the meals and the people. Ownership changed a few times and my Rotary Club met there for a few years before it closed permanently and our town lost an institution.

In those days there were two great record stores where many of us hung out after school. Before the Internet, we bought and collected vinyl records as soon as they came out.

My sister and I got along well with the staff at the funeral home. Carl Steele, who had been with us since he was a teenager, often played football with me in the parking lot. He coached me for the Punt, Pass and Kick competition. The stripes in the parking lot made it easy to duplicate a football field.

We also had a great sporting goods store on Calhoun Street two blocks behind the funeral home. Jack Pearl's was a frequent hangout and I spent a small fortune there.

Calhoun Street was once a thriving little block near the high school. Not only did it have Jack Pearl's, but Goode's Bakery. I often was sent over to pick up doughnuts and rolls for visitations at the funeral home. Even better was the presence of Henry's Ice Cream Shop. It was an old-fashioned store with wood benches. It was a classic malt shop out of the "Happy Days" television show. They made all the ice cream fresh and it was a frequent after-school stop. We never had a family gathering where we didn't pick up a few half-gallons of ice cream to take along. Their lemon ice cream was a favorite and hasn't been matched anywhere since.

Jack Harkness, who ran the shop until it closed in the early 1980s, always wore a paper hat and white apron and kept good track of which kids he needed to keep an eye on. One day we had a half-day of school and several of us headed over to Henry's for ice cream when school let out. Mr. Harkness refused to serve us because he thought we were skipping school. That's the way things were in those days.

As I got older I ended up doing chores at the funeral home. One of the biggest jobs was washing cars. We had a fleet that included a hearse, two limousines and our station wagon. I spent hours after school washing and getting them ready for the next day. This is where I learned to love taking care of cars and I took pride in the appearance of our fleet. Still to this day I cannot stand driving a dirty car and every car I've owned has looked new going into six-digit mileage.

Of course, I also mowed the lawn. We had a very small patch of grass in front of the funeral home and I expanded my employment to the neighbors' lawns around us, making a few extra dollars. I shoveled walks in winter and did routine maintenance around the funeral home, often moving caskets and setting up chairs for services. All of it was very typical for any kid who grew up in a funeral home.

For many years one of our biggest suppliers of caskets was Marsellus Casket Company of Syracuse, New York. Marsellus, a fourth-generation family business, was the premier wood casket maker in America for years. The load came by semi and I often helped unload the truck and get the caskets to the basement and onto the selection floor.

On many occasions, the driver knew I was taking shop class. He often brought me pieces of scrap wood from the factory, including pieces of mahogany and walnut. I got brownie points from my wood shop teacher when I walked in with the premium scrap wood. I still have a mahogany lamp I made with pieces of Marsellus wood.

When my dad died, John Marsellus, who my parents got to know at conventions and funeral events, called us when he heard. He oversaw the production of a Marsellus President mahogany casket for us and even had them do a special tailoring with French blue velvet that wasn't available in standard production. Marsellus also made a substantial contribution to his and my dad's shared passion of Ducks Unlimited. We will always be grateful. A few years later when the company finally closed and was acquired by a conglomerate, the funeral business lost a standard of excellence that will never be repeated. I wrote a column on the Marsellus Company's demise that was published in many of the funeral business journals.

When I was in high school, the third-floor apartment made for close quarters living. The family room was just outside my bedroom and I often had difficulty falling asleep as Dad crashed on the sofa watching television after a long day. Many times I got up at 11:30 and lay down in front of the TV and watched the entire "Tonight Show with Johnny Carson" while dad slept. When it was over, I'd wake him up and tell him to go to bed. I saw nearly every episode of the "Tonight Show" during its prime years.

Dad never knew it, but I often snuck down to the garage late at night and took the station wagon out for a spin without anyone noticing. I usually ended up about a mile away at the 7-Eleven for a Slurpee, and I cruised by friends' houses before returning to the garage. I often did this on a learner's permit. I was lucky I never got stopped.

Later when we all got our licenses we would often take our family station wagons out. A friend, Kevin Christ, always wanted to race, but I usually resisted because it was a business car. Once he took off next to me at a stop light and I let him go. A few minutes later he was pulled over by police as I drove by. Those were the days.

Living in tight quarters and at the funeral home taught me a lot about the business world. Looking back, I marvel at the sacrifices my parents made by living at the office, saving money and working hard. By being at the funeral home 24 hours a day, seven days a week my dad could do paperwork in the evening, come up and have dinner and go back and finish. We were always there for families and could stay on top of everything going on. Despite living in cramped quarters, it was a great life!

Lesson Learned

Having to move from a comfortable neighborhood with lots of friends was a challenge. Having to make new friends was also a challenge, but everything worked out. We only moved across town, but many families move across the country, many times, and never really know where home is. It taught us that change is a constant and the younger we learn that lesson the better.

I've always been intrigued by military children who follow their parents around the country or world to new assignments. I wondered how they do it, never really having roots. It seems they are never anywhere long enough to develop solid, lasting friendships and are constantly the new kid on the block. One military colleague I once talked with said he treasures the opportunities he had as a child and all the places he's seen and been. Many friends weren't really friends at all, he told me, but he stayed close to those he liked. I assume that today the Internet and social media make it easier to stay connected with childhood friends.

If anyone can **Defy the Immediate** it has to be military kids. Many never live anywhere more than two years, but they embrace the nomadic life and are better for it. They teach us that dealing with change is a given in life and they accept the challenges it brings. Always remember that military families and especially military kids make as many sacrifices as their parents do. Their life is all about change.

CHAPTER 4

College Years – Chippewas:
We're Proud of Our Nickname

"Education is what remains after one has forgotten what one has learned in school."
— Albert Einstein

Beginning around the middle of junior year, college-bound high school students realize it's time to get serious about where they will head after graduation and what they will do for the rest of their lives. It can be a frightening time.

I grew up in a University of Michigan family. We attended all the home football games in Ann Arbor, parked in the same lot for three generations, more than 45 years, and even went to a few Rose Bowls. Obviously, my first thought and natural choice was Michigan. My dad's side of the family was all true blue. His father attended Michigan and both his brothers were proud graduates.

I applied to Michigan and was probably laughed out of the admissions office when they saw my application. The rejection came quickly and I realized I wasn't even competitive.

Four years later, my sister Elizabeth had better luck, eventually graduating from the College of Literature, Science and the Arts. Years later she received LSA's Distinguished Alumni Award and became the first female president of the University of Michigan Club of Chicago. She was my dad's pride and joy.

After my U of M dream vanished, I decided Michigan State (God forbid!) would be my target. In my family that was like renouncing your citizenship, but my parents were pleased and supportive. My dad even went with me to an admissions interview in East Lansing, a difficult experience for him. The interview was routine and perfunctory. I didn't feel good about it and was overwhelmed by the size of the school. I didn't think it was for me and I was right.

Then, early in my senior year, I was selected to attend a seminar for high school journalists at Central Michigan University. The Michigan Interscholastic Press Association puts on an event each year where young journalists come to CMU and learn about journalism as a career and get to work on a newspaper that is published at the end of the seminar. It was a blast, and I ended up writing a feature in the paper and getting interested in CMU's journalism program. I learned that CMU had a highly regarded journalism school and an award-winning student newspaper – Central Michigan LIFE. This one event told me that CMU was the right choice for me. It was two hours from home, far enough away, and it had everything I needed to pursue my career choice.

I applied and was quickly accepted. I was ecstatic and couldn't wait to start classes. CMU was a comfortable setting for me – small enough to feel part of, but big enough to have the amenities of a large institution. In hindsight, it was the perfect choice.

Close family friend Harry Boesch was one of the reasons I decided to study journalism. He was in corporate communications at Kellogg and knew I loved to write. One night on our dock at Gull Lake he told me I couldn't go wrong pursuing journalism because the ability to communicate well was important in any occupation. His words reaffirmed the direction I was already leaning.

In high school, I went on a drama club trip to New York with classmates. Harry tried to get me tickets through Kellogg to see "Saturday Night Live," which was in its infancy. Unfortunately, he learned there was no live show the weekend we were there. We were all disappointed not to get a chance to see John Belushi, Gilda Radner and the other original cast members.

In August 1978 I attended a summer orientation at CMU and spent a night in "the Towers," the eight-story dorm. I met other incoming freshmen from all around Michigan, making friendships we'd rekindle when we returned to campus in the fall. At the orientation, we took tests that revealed my substandard math skills. No surprise there. A remedial math class helped, but I still struggled.

My parents drove me to campus for the move-in to the dorms. My room was on the third floor of Thorpe Hall, right across from CMU's Kelly/Shorts Stadium and Rose Arena, the basketball venue. I soon learned that Thorpe Hall was the "jock dorm" because of its proximity to the sports venues. It was an all-male dorm that shared a connection to Beddow Hall, the female dorm.

I lucked out and got into the two-man side of the five-man room. In those days, baby boomers swelled the dorms and freshmen squeezed five to a room. My roommate was Jon Twing, from White Cloud, Michigan. His father was an executive with the Gerber baby food company in nearby Fremont. Jon was a big guy and played football at White Cloud. He told me they had a very small team and he played offense and defense in every play of every game in high school. White Cloud won their final game his senior year and the town went crazy; it was the highlight of his year. He was invited as a walk-on to CMU's team, but declined in order to focus on academics. Today, Dr. Twing is an educational consultant in Iowa.

Thorpe was a rowdy dorm and on the first night of classes everyone was hanging out in the halls getting to know each other, when I guess "the boys decided to be boys". All of a sudden, we were storming Beddow in an old-fashioned panty raid. I followed the guys through the halls as the Beddow resident assistants tried to stand their ground and demanded that we leave. We assembled outside Beddow Hall and everyone began shouting "panties! panties!" and women were throwing panties out their windows. It was hilarious. College was going to be fun!

One of the residents of Beddow Hall was Amy Roloff, who was born with a type of dwarfism called achalasia. She went on to fame and celebrity with her family in TLC's "Little People, Big World" television show. A few years ago, she returned to CMU as grand marshal of homecoming.

My freshman year started uneventfully and I made friends easily. I especially enjoyed the journalism classes. My advisor, by fate, was Suzanne Nichols, a journalism professor. I soon learned she had graduated from high school in Battle Creek and was one of my dad's classmates. She was a great advisor and knew journalism well. In the first reporting class I took from her, she drilled in *"Accuracy, accuracy, accuracy!"* Our work was often brutally edited and given back to us – me included. Many students became frustrated and dropped her class. I apparently took the right attitude and learned from it. She complimented me on my improvement, but was totally honest when my work was subpar. She was one of the reasons CMU's journalism program was so well regarded.

A few weeks after school started and I got settled into the routine, I ventured into the LIFE office and applied to be a reporter. After a few weeks of seeing how the operation worked I became a full-fledged staff writer. We were beyond the archaic term of "reporter" in those days. Staff Writer was part of your byline and it meant you got paid by the inch for every story.

The upperclassmen were the seasoned editors and spent many hours working on the paper, which was published Mondays, Wednesdays and Fridays during the semester. We all worked on special fall and spring tabloids. In the fall, it was the Homecoming tabloid and near spring break, the annual Car Care guide. It was almost a full-time job for them and I always wondered how they found time for classes.

When you became a staff writer, you got a square on the bulletin board in the newsroom where the editors posted notes and story assignments. I came by several times a day to see if I had any assignments.

Finally, I got one. I needed to contact the head of the Central Michigan Democrats and write a story about their efforts to draft Ted Kennedy for the 1980 presidential election. It was a little out of my comfort zone, at least politically, but that's how you learn. I set up a meeting with the head of the group and we had a good discussion about why they thought Kennedy would make a great president. Kennedy would have to wrest the Democratic nomination away from President Jimmy Carter, a daunting task, to appear on the ballot. I spent some time crafting the story, getting good quotes, doing what I'd recently learned in my journalism classes and turned in the story. I typed it on a Smith-Corona manual typewriter using carbon paper for two copies. You had to self-edit the work with proper editing marks before you turned it in. I was lucky the editors never had to do a major overhaul of my work; usually they called me over to go over style issues and how better to phrase things. I was gaining a good reputation as a freshman writer and with it came more story assignments.

"Draft Kennedy" was my first front page byline story. It ran – in newspaper language – below the fold (the bottom half of the page). Still, it was a moral victory and fired me up.

I soon was getting a story in nearly every issue. As a reward, I was assigned to cover the police beat. I had to visit the Department of Public Safety (DPS) each day and look over the log for possible good stories. It wasn't easy. On top of that, the campus police weren't exactly helpful. I tried to be friendly while the police officers were matter-of-fact and not very engaging.

I did get to do a ride-along one night after a football game. The police mostly broke up fights and responded to brawls. I discovered that many of the troublemakers on campus were high school students from other areas coming over to party. I also learned that the cops wore heavy, weighted gloves, essentially wearable sandbags, when breaking up fights. Who says life is fair?

One of the most exciting moments came when we were driving across campus and a car blew through an intersection and bottomed out in front of us. It was dark and you could see the sparks fly. Lights and a siren came on and we pulled the car over. Once again, they were high schoolers out thinking they were big shots. The officer I rode with said, *"Looks like I might have to write them up for 'illegal cultivation of pavement!'"* We chuckled, and a little while later he dropped me off at my dorm and I began working on a story.

By the end of that first semester, I phased out of the police beat and asked for something different. I wrote feature stories about faculty members' Christmas traditions. I found a history professor who was a model train enthusiast. The story was well received and much more fun than trying to get scraps from the DPS.

In the spring, I got the Greek beat, covering the campus fraternities and sororities. It seemed like a lot of fun and I got to know many of the Greek leaders on campus.

One of my editors suggested I write a piece on what it was like to go through Rush, the formal recruitment period when you visit Greek houses and look over prospective fraternities you might join.

I didn't have a strong opinion about fraternities at that point. What I knew came from the men in my family, most of whom were in fraternities. But it was a different time when they attended college.

As fate would have it, one of my roommates got an invitation to a Sigma Chi party. I knew a little about the fraternity because one of my dad's best friends, Joe Schwarz, was a Sigma Chi and I knew Sigma Chi was the best-known fraternity in the world, sort of the Rotary Club of fraternities. I also knew that the famous song "Sweetheart of Sigma Chi" was penned at Albion College near Battle Creek.

My roommate wasn't really interested, so I picked up the invite and called the Rush chairman and asked if I could come. I felt I needed to let them know that I was a reporter doing a story. I talked with the fraternity president, Dan Klekner, and Rush chairman Dar Morgan and explained I was a LIFE reporter doing a feature on Rush. I told him I didn't want to be treated any differently than an average student. In hindsight, what a mistake! The entire fraternity was in on the gig and I got the royal treatment. I was picked up at my dorm room by two tall skinny guys, Don Fergle and Jon Ketelhut, who were wearing polyester, hip-hugger pants and leather jackets and looked like they'd just stepped off the set of the disco movie "Saturday Night Fever." My first thought: What was I in for?

We got to the party and it was rocking. Everyone in the fraternity went out of their way to get to know me; even the sorority girls were interested in me. Remember, I was still a young, impressionable freshman. I had one of the best times of my life and felt a little guilty about it because I was there on assignment. I was totally impressed with Sigma Chi and made friends with many of the brothers.

I also attended a few other fraternity Rush parties for perspective. Honestly, none of them compared to Sigma Chi. I covered the Bid Day event when they gave bids to students to become pledges. Every fraternity stood around a big platform on Warriner Mall and all the rushees were called to the platform for the announcement of what fraternity they've chosen. They then dove into the crowd, like a scene at a rock concert. I don't think they do that anymore as schools have become sensitive about injuries and political correctness. Still, it was a great tradition.

I put Sigma Chi in the back of my mind and concentrated on getting through the spring semester. As the Greek reporter, it wasn't a good idea to get too involved with one group. But Sigma Chi was a real possibility for the following fall.

I wrote many more features about Greek life the rest of the semester. I just happened to be at a Greek Week event when we heard about a fire at the Sigma Pi house. I rushed out, and saw the house engulfed and put on my reporter hat. I talked with many of the brothers, got quotes, rushed back to the newsroom and put together a big news story along with another reporter. It was front page news for a few weeks and I did several follow-ups and talked with contractors and fraternity members about the future of the house. It ended up one of the biggest campus stories of the year.

Although hard news is the bread and butter of journalism, I enjoyed feature story reporting and writing much more. I especially liked not having deadline pressure.

Each spring, just before spring break, CM LIFE published a Car Care tabloid. It was a great tradition and really fun to work on. I LOVE CARS. I did a feature on gasohol, which at that time was an experimental concept in fuel additives where grain alcohol is added to gasoline for environmental and economic benefits. Today it's ethanol or E-85. I did my research and discovered that the only distributor of gasohol in Michigan was a farm elevator in nearby Breckenridge. I called the manager and set up an interview, took an afternoon and learned all about gasohol. Breckenridge is in the heart of soybean country and the alcohol was being made from the byproducts of corn and soy bean processing. The story almost wrote itself.

The fuel distributor told me he had heard that the Jack Daniels Distillery in Lynchburg, Tennessee, was doing the same thing with their byproducts. Of course, I followed up on that and called Jack Daniels after I got back to the newsroom. For a college newspaper, that would be an interesting angle! After getting the runaround, I finally talked with someone in the distillery's public relations department. He didn't know what I was talking about, but it was fun trying to track down the rumor. I wish I had told him that my dad was a huge fan of Jack Daniels and asked if I could get some free samples or promotional gear. But it just didn't seem professional.

The story was one of the top features in the tabloid and was highlighted on the front cover. The editors had hoped the tabloid would be a contender in their annual submission for the Pacemaker Award, which honors the best college newspapers in the country. CM LIFE has won many Pacemakers. Unfortunately, the editors misspelled GASAHOL in the big letters of a headline on the cover of the tabloid. The staff was devastated, knowing that after all the work that went into the tabloid, it wouldn't and couldn't contend for a Pacemaker.

Much of the success of CM LIFE can be credited to journalism professor

The author in 1979 with Washington Post Executive Editor Ben Bradlee in the CM Life office, where Shaw worked while at Central Michigan University. Shaw was Bradlee's tour guide and introduced the famous newspaper editor before Bradlee's speech to students. (CM Life photo)

and publications advisor Jim Wojcik. His influence on the paper was profound. Woj not only kept the staff focused on the journalism mission but often went to bat for students when administrators had concerns about what was being reported. He'd remind them that the student paper was protected by the first amendment and independent of the school. CM LIFE was the watchdog of the university and he made sure student journalists took that role seriously and professionally. Woj also had an incredible network of media connections around the state and Midwest and helped many journalists land their first jobs and in their careers. Most of the Lifers have remained friends with Wojcik over the years.

Another great opportunity was dropped in my lap that semester. I was asked by the head of University Events if I would like to pick up guest speaker

Ben Bradlee at the airport in Midland in March. Bradlee, then executive editor of the Washington Post and key figure in the Watergate saga, was coming to CMU as part of the speakers' series. I jumped at the opportunity!

The first thing I did was extensive research. I wanted to be able to chat intelligently with him on the hour ride from the airport. As a young journalist he was very close to President John F. Kennedy. I found his book, "Conversations with Kennedy," and read it.

As the day arrived, University Events asked me to also be Bradlee's escort. That meant being with him most of the day and making sure he got to all his appointments and meetings, mostly with journalism students and faculty and a few parties in the evening. Once again, I was thrilled.

Then came the real kicker. I was asked, since I'd done so much research, if I'd introduce him to the audience at his speech in Warriner Hall. Wow! Of course, I said, "Absolutely!"

I sat next to him on stage and when the time came, I stood in front of more than 1,000 people and introduced Ben Bradlee. His speech was entitled "To Print or Not to Print!" and dealt with the issues of responsible reporting, privacy and legality.

Although I was somewhat nervous looking over the big crowd of students, faculty and friends, I took a deep breath and read my prepared introduction, which included Bradlee's experiences with JFK and Watergate. I ended my remarks by introducing his topic – editorial conundrums. My parents drove up from Battle Creek for the event and I was told they cried seeing me up there. I sat back down and took notes throughout the speech while enjoying the audience's rapt attention to Bradlee.

At that time there was no internet, blogging or instant communication. The information age was in its infancy and the major media – newspapers and television – were still the gatekeepers of information and bore a huge responsibility for what should and shouldn't be reported. The world has changed dramatically since then.

Much of Bradlee's speech was about Watergate and his star reporters Bob Woodward and Carl Bernstein. Their coverage of the entire saga eventually led to the resignation of President Richard M. Nixon in August 1974.

At that time the identity of "Deep Throat," the critical anonymous source in the Watergate scandal, remained a mystery. When someone from the audience asked about Deep Throat – they always do in the question and answer session – Bradlee responded, *"I'm afraid that's going to have to remain Washington's best-kept secret!"* The person then asked, *"Can you tell us anything about him?"* Bradlee quickly responded, *"Him?"* The audience roared and the speech ended.

In May 2005 Mark Felt, former associate director of the FBI, was revealed as Deep Throat, ending 30 years of speculation and intrigue.

When Bradlee visited several journalism classes at CMU, one of the things that stuck with me was his vision of the future of the craft. He said that while it was rapidly changing, reporting all the facts with truthfulness and objectivity would always be paramount.

But the admonition Bradlee gave that sticks with me most was: *"Learn Chinese."* He was right on the money!

Lesson Learned

Journalism seemed easy for me and I found my voice in writing. The faculty challenged me enough that I improved with each story. Getting involved with the college newspaper got me out and about on campus and raised my curiosity about everything. If anything, journalism teaches you to look deeper at everything. Some skepticism is a good thing. As is intellectual honesty and integrity in what you report.

My improvement as a writer helped me in every other aspect of college. My freshman year was one of my best and set the stage for the rest of my college career. I became a team player on the newspaper staff. Without knowing it at the time, I **Defied the Immediate** and rose above the crowd, made a name for myself and grew in every aspect of my life. The lesson here is that you don't need permission to be exceptional, you just have to act like it and work toward it.

College can be one of the most frightening times in a young person's life. It's a huge transition from leaving a secure home and family and the first real step to making your way in the world. I was fortunate I landed at a great institution where the environment made the transition easier. It was hard at first, but as each day grew, new challenges presented themselves. There were academic and social challenges, having to deal with roommate issues and making new friends. You soon learned that everyone was in the same boat emotionally. Making friends came easily. As I began taking classes my intellectual curiosity grew.

CHAPTER 5

——

Outward Bound – to Serve, to Strive and Not to Yield!

"All life demands struggle. Those who have everything given to them become lazy, selfish, and insensitive to the real values of life. The very striving and hard work that we so constantly try to avoid is the major building block in the person we are today."

— Pope Paul VI

In high school I watched a National Geographic special about a program that took underachieving urban youth to the mountains of Colorado where they faced a progression of leadership challenges. The goal was to make these troubled kids better people by confronting and overcoming obstacles, often using teamwork. I was fascinated.

The program was Outward Bound, which has a rich history of creating leaders by dropping them in tough wilderness situations. Think quasi-military survival school. After thorough investigation, I wanted to give it a shot. The idea of creating rugged individuals by challenging personal abilities and endurance, something I saw being lost in our society, was appealing.

After my freshman college year, I needed something to boost my confidence and outlook. I applied to the Colorado Outward Bound School and was thrilled when I was accepted for a three-week course in the high country. It was new territory for me, but I saw the challenge as something that would help me succeed in college and beyond.

Their precourse mailings outlined physical prerequisites, including the ability to run at least three miles. I had never run three miles in my life. It wasn't easy, but at that age you can still do remarkable physical things.

The time came to head to Colorado. We met up in the little town of Gunnison near the San Juan and Uncompahgre Range where we'd be hiking the next few days.

On the bus ride to base camp, the leaders chatted with us individually and tried to discern everyone's level of fitness and outdoor experience level. Many were already good mountaineers and accomplished outdoorsmen and women.

I had little outdoor experience beyond some Boy Scout camping. I had never been in high country, and had done no rock climbing or mountaineering. I did do some rappelling with the Army ROTC unit at CMU, so I knew a little about it.

They wanted to have groups, or patrols, of 10 made up of a good mix of talent. It was soon apparent I was in the "green" group made of many like me with little or no experience. This was going to be interesting.

The leaders of Outward Bound were seasoned trainers and mountaineers. Dodie Udall, the overall course leader, was a bit of a celebrity and had been with Outward Bound for a few years. This was her first opportunity as a full-fledged course leader, overseeing the four patrols. If her last name sounds familiar, she is the daughter of the late Rep. Morris Udall from Arizona. The Udall family is well-known in Western politics. Her brother Mark Udall was also an instructor and became Outward Bound's executive director before serving as a congressman and U.S. senator from Colorado. For Dodie, shepherding our group was a big step in her Outward Bound career.

At base camp we were briefed and grouped with our patrols. We were issued backpacks and supplies and learned how to pack them so they would be balanced and easier to carry. We divided up food and supplies with everyone responsible for something for the group. It was June and the weather was fantastic, but – like Michigan's – it can change quickly and dramatically.

We had to prepare for everything. The weather can range from scorching heat to near freezing in hours at that time of year. They recommended wool clothing. Fortunately, I also invested in a good pair of hiking boots and several pairs of wool socks. In Michigan, we had few expedition stores selling mountaineering gear, so I went to a local clothing store, Ratti & Sons, that specialized in military surplus merchandise. I told them I needed a really good pair of wool pants and shirts for mountaineering. What I got was a very heavy pair of wool dress pants that I assumed would be what I needed. They were comfortable and would fit over a pair of jeans or khakis when it got cold and wet. I thought they were perfect. I had a few Pendleton wool shirts, which also worked well. I ended up wearing the wool pants almost every day of the expedition. Everyone laughed that I was overdressed, but the pants were warm. After 21 days, they were in shreds!

Once we got our packs loaded, we learned how to properly put them on our backs and balance them. Although heavy, they were comfortable, but it still took time to get used to them.

One of the first and most critical things we learned was to stay hydrated. There are many wild animals in the high country and any water source, no matter how clear, is suspect for bacteria and microorganisms. We were given bottles of iodine to treat water we collected from pristine streams and snowmelt. It took a while to get used to the taste of iodized water, but better safe than sick. Ticks were a worry, too, and we did frequent tick checks on each other.

After lots of basic training we were ready. Our instructor and guide was Jerry Roberts, a rugged outdoorsman who called himself Rev. Roberts. We believed he had religious credentials for tax purposes. Nevertheless, he was a great guide and mentor. He was constantly challenging us, as he should have, and chewed us out when he needed to. He was almost a drill sergeant and stayed on us for everything. We quickly learned that we needed to do things right and as a team if we were going to make it through the next few weeks. Teamwork was paramount!

Since this experience was new, we didn't get far the first day before we set up camp. We learned to appreciate camp food, as most of it was high energy. We learned techniques for cooking and preparing what we had. Every few days we were resupplied with food at predetermined points. There is little natural food in the high country in early summer, especially above the tree line, where we spent a lot of time.

One of our first challenges was crossing a swift stream. We came to a downed tree just at water level that would be our bridge. The tree was laced with ice, so it was treacherous. We had to gain confidence sidestepping across it or we would fall in with full backpacks. Everyone made it, some with a little help. Our first real challenge was in the books!

Our biorhythms got into sync with the sun. We were up at daylight and typically started with a lot of energy and excitement. By night, we were dead tired and slept well regardless of comfort level. We didn't have tents, just tarps we rigged between trees to keep the dew off us. It was more important to have a barrier below us than above us; we all had a sheet of plastic and a rollup mat and got used to it. The plastic sheets were rolled up over our sleeping bags to keep them dry during the day and attached to the bottom of the backpack. Dry sleeping bags, or "fart sacks" as we called them, were a real comfort at night.

Keeping your boots warm was also a challenge. When we slept at night, our boots were placed in our sleeping bags right behind our knees. It kept them dry and warm. Still, when I got up in the morning, they were never as warm as I would have liked them, but our motto was to "start cold" because you warm up as you move. Starting cold was never a problem.

During our first week we hiked above the tree line and into snow. This is where we first went to "snow school" and learned to walk and cross snow fields. As a group, we learned to "post hole" where we walked in a line stepping in everyone's tracks. Each of us had an ice axe. It was our most useful tool, especially in the snow. It's about three feet long with a point on the end. The top head has a spike on one side and a flat chisel on other. If we were ever to fall and slide, proper use of the axe could save our lives. We were shown how to stop a slide by laying on the axe, digging our toes in and using the spiked head as a brake. We all had to become proficient in stopping a slide before we could proceed.

When you descended a mountain, if the snow conditions were right, you could glissade down the slope. You just sat down, started sliding and used your heels and your ice axe point as a rudder. It was a blast, especially if you could slide several thousand feet while keeping control. We could only do this where there was no possibility of an avalanche. In June, the snow is hard and somewhat icy and there is little chance of starting an avalanche.

The next day, we would begin our first ascent of one of the peaks in the Uncompahgre Range.

The day of our climb was beautiful and sunny as we began the 3,000 foot climb to the summit of Wetterhorn Peak which sits at 14,000 feet above sea level…a respectable climb.

The air is thin and crisp above the timberline. As the sun rose, we grabbed breakfast and started up the mountain. Soon we were in snow and ice and the climbing was difficult. Many times I lost footing and slid, but my ice axe saved me. I kept getting back up. It was purposely slow for a reason: At upward of 10,000 feet, oxygen levels drop and many of us were gasping for air. We took frequent breaks.

About three hours into the adventure, the summit was in sight and we grew excited. The sun was bright and if it was cold, we didn't feel it. Eventually, euphoria overcame us – *"We're here!"* We had reached the summit. It was apparently a popular destination; a large rock cairn greeted us at the top. We all signed a log book in the cairn as testament to our accomplishment. We sat around for a long time taking in the view. In the distance we could see Gunnison and Durango, Colorado and the Rocky Mountain Range was breathtakingly beautiful under a cloudless clear blue sky.

We had lunch before reluctantly starting our descent. I soon discovered that descending is harder than climbing. If you put your foot down too hard, it is easy to slip and lose footing. Gravity is unforgiving and wants to pull you down. Going up, there was some resistance, but going down was more treacherous and dangerous. Many of us were also tired, so we had to look out for each other and work as a team.

As the days went on, we became more and more confident. We climbed a few more peaks, including Pole Creek and Wood Mountain.

One day we did rock climbing – a challenge for me. The best climbers went first. Once at the top, we tended our ropes to help each other up. The person at the top was only there for safety to save you if you fell or slipped. They kept the rope taut, they didn't pull you up. Once you made it up the rock, you had to help the next climber. I watched others ascend about 100 feet, but once you were halfway up you started overthinking it and had to fight back fear.

For me it was terribly difficult to find grips and footholds, I slipped many times, greatly burdening the person at the top. The instructors helped by telling me where to grab onto the rocks, but I could never get a confident grip and my toe holds kept slipping. It took a massive amount of positive attitude, relaxing and really thinking and concentrating, but I finally made it and helped the next person up.

After a few weeks of progressive confidence building, we had to do a solo – three days and two nights in the wilderness on our own. Everyone in the patrol was given an area they had to stay in. In reality we weren't very far apart, but we were not to wander from our base. We had no food, but that wasn't a problem. The purpose of this was introspection and reflection.

Every morning we had to build a rock pile, a cairn, near the trail so the instructors knew we were alright. I found out later that they kept a pretty close eye on us, although we never saw them. They were stealthy.

I was placed on a stream, near a trail. The first day was very relaxing. I made myself comfortable, took in the surroundings, wrote in my journal, crawled into my sleeping bag and slept soundly through the night. It was a break from the demands of our training. I didn't get up until well past sunrise the next morning, stretched and went to the stream for water and got comfortable again, dozing and thinking about all I had been through. I became hypersensitive to everything around me, the sound of the stream, the stirring of the wind, the glare of the sun and everything else. Fortunately it never rained, which was wonderful. All I had was the tarp and my gear to keep me dry. It never really got very cold, but the sleeping bag provided great warmth. I may have made a small fire.

I slept fairly well the second night, but hunger was starting to gnaw at me. I drank plenty of water, but it never really satisfied me. I knew this would end soon. There was nothing I could do about it.

It was early on the second morning when I really had my epiphany. I woke up with a lot of very deep thoughts about my life, what I'd done and where I was going. The emotions of the moment were overwhelming and I began crying uncontrollably. A few minutes later, my heart began racing and felt like it was going to jump out of my chest. It scared me as I was overcome with fear about what was happening. Then, all of a sudden, a calmness came over me, and my heartbeat returned to normal.

I felt a warm sensation all over my body. It was like I had achieved total relaxation. I was not sure if I had just experienced a physiological or spiritual event, or a combination. From that moment on, I felt great, I felt empowered and I felt a confidence I'd never had before. It was like I was recharged and reclaimed.

A few hours later Jerry Roberts came and got me and rounded everyone up. We ate and shared our experiences. I talked about a heightened sense of awareness and the beauty of our surroundings, but was reluctant to talk about my spiritual experience. It was definitely the highlight of the course for me and galvanized my resolve to make the most of my life, regardless of what challenges I faced.

After the solo expedition, the course wound down. All four patrols came together for a few days to bond, share experiences and have one-on-ones with the instructors to talk about what we learned. I sat down with Roberts. I don't remember much about our discussion, but I do remember that at one point I cried, realizing that I had completed a course I had feared I'd fail. His encouragement and positivity lifted my spirits and made me stronger.

During the day we built a sauna with all the tarps and made a giant teepee. We heated rocks in a fire and brought them into the tent and splashed them with water. We felt great sweating out all our dirt and grime. We then jumped into a cold stream. It was awesome. We had a big feast that evening and all sat around a campfire like old friends and laughed the night away. I'm not sure if we slept or not, but the next morning the bus came to take us back to Gunnison and civilization.

It was truly a life-changing experience.

The only downside to this great adventure came a week after I returned home. We had always been very careful about treating our drinking and cooking water, but I later learned that using iodine isn't always completely effective. I contracted a horrible delayed case of giardiasis, a diarrheal disease that affects your lower GI tract in a considerable way, and eventually had to get some serious medication. I was in misery.

I called our family friend, Dr. Joe Schwarz, an otolaryngologist or ear, nose and throat specialist, who gave me a diarrhea prescription that did little to nothing to alleviate the problem. A few days later my friend's dad, Dr. Vance Lancaster, an internist and avid skier who has spent considerable time in Colorado, heard about my plight and called me. When I told him that Joe had given me this specific anti-diarrhea prescription, he said *"That doesn't work!"* He called in a stronger prescription that worked effectively in less than 24 hours. I was relieved!

When he called in a few days to check up on me he said that giardiasis is common in Colorado and that he knew all about it. Then he said, *"I'm glad you're feeling better, but next time you've got a problem with your ass, don't call a head doctor!"* We both laughed and I thanked him again. Sage advice from a good friend who knew what I was going through!

Lesson Learned

Attending the Colorado Outward Bound School took an enormous amount of courage for me. I can't say I was in the best or strongest patrol, but we came together to meet the progressive challenges we faced, learned a lot about ourselves and became better people for it. The entire curriculum is built on facing the next challenge. I had more than my share of self-doubting moments.

It was a real life-changing event few people get to experience. It proved to me, and all of us, that we are better than we realize, and that we must demand more of ourselves.

We learned that we are often our own worst enemies and that when we look back, the task and objective weren't really as hard as we imagined. This is a great parable and applicable to most everything in life. Everything looks easier in hindsight. We are greater than what we imagine, and fear and anxiety are phantoms that get in the way of our success.

Throughout our three-week trek in the Colorado high country there were many times we had to **Defy the Immediate**, both individually and as a team, and we all came through and survived. It wasn't always easy, but with perseverance and teamwork we did it. We all left the course better than when we started, and for me I had a new sense of confidence and determination to be the very best me I could be.

CHAPTER 6

Pledging Sigma Chi

"In westerns, you meet a hardy bunch of characters. There is no jealousy on such pictures."
— John Wayne (Sigma Chi, University of Southern California)

The summer after my Outward Bound experience I decided to pledge Sigma Chi, a decision I made in the high country of Colorado where there was time to think about such cerebral things.

Early in my sophomore year I still worked for CM LIFE and did feature stories, although it wasn't a priority. I loved writing, but hard news wasn't my forte. Most of my stories weren't time sensitive and that gave me more time for classwork and pledging.

It wasn't a sure thing, but Sigma Chi really wanted me. I attended other rush parties and also received a bid from rival Sigma Pi. I had made several friends working with Sigma Pi on their fire recovery story but there was no doubt Sigma Chi was the only choice for me. I was honored when they extended me a bid to pledge the legendary fraternity.

Bid day, a tradition on CMU's campus, is an exciting event. All the rushees who have received bids gather and then are called up on a platform by name and asked who they've selected. The fraternities are gathered all around the platform and don't know who'll accept their bid. You are then asked who you will pledge; you rush over to your group and literally dive into brotherhood like a mosh pit at a concert. You get thrown in the air a few times and are welcomed to the group. It was a lot of fun, but unfortunately that tradition has vanished for liability reasons. We've become wimps and overly cautious and litigious. Today, bid day is much more subdued. Political correctness strikes again!

While stories abound about how pledges are hazed, a cruel form of humiliation and abuse under the guise of "tradition," I never saw any of it. In fact, Sigma Chi was a leader in abolishing hazing. During my time in the fraternity, our national board required us to post a prominent anti-hazing policy statement in our house. In the first few pledge meetings, it was drilled in that hazing had no place in the fraternity. It was refreshing to hear that hazing was the quickest way to lose our charter and was not a way to create character and leadership. I grew more impressed with the fraternity all the time.

During the time I was pledging, the Interfraternity Council hosted a lecture by Eileen Stevens, the mother of a college student who died in 1978 in a hazing incident. Her son, Chuck Stenzel, a freshman at Alfred University in New York, died in the trunk of a car from hypothermia and acute alcohol poisoning at the hands of a fraternity gone wild. Her crusade and organization CHUCK (Committee to Halt Useless College Killings) was powerful and well received. It was her personal crusade, and she has shared her message at more than 700 colleges through the years.

Some of the things we did during pledging were frowned upon by our national as potential hazing. One of the most memorable pledging traditions in our chapter involved carrying a huge log.

We met at a park outside of town and all the pledges had to join to pick up a log and carry it down the path, all working together to carry one another and the chapter. As we proceeded down the trail and struggled, our big brothers (active mentors) stepped in to lighten the load. A little farther down the path, the rest of the brothers stepped in to help and the burden became very light. Once we got to the end of the trail, we had a bonfire and had great discussions on pulling together as a class and a chapter and "carrying the log." It was enlightening, symbolic and powerful.

The funny story about the log carry came after we were given our instructions. We were all silent when we started to lift the log. It was supposed to be a silent, thoughtful and reflective exercise. I bent over to help pick it up, but we just had too many of us on one side of the log, so I stepped over the log to lift from the other side. Just as I stepped over, everyone else picked it up with me straddling it. We were on silence, so no one could say anything. For a moment, I was riding the log with all my pledge brothers carrying me and not sure what I should do because we couldn't speak. I extended my arm and said "Onward!" like a trail boss. A moment later I swung my other leg over and slid off on the opposite side and started carrying it. Others around me saw what had happened and struggled hard to not burst out laughing. Needless to say, I took a lot of grief for that, but we all roared over it later. It was a bonding moment and was just one of those great and humbling experiences that create character! Unfortunately, the log carry was deemed a dangerous exercise and potentially hazing, so a great CMU tradition went by the wayside.

We were told that pledging should be considered an additional class because there was a lot to learn. Each week we had quizzes and tests on the history, rules and traditions of the fraternity and Greek life in general. It took time, effort and dedication, but it was all worth it.

Sigma Chi has a great history and I loved history. I studied the founders and the leaders the fraternity has produced. I also dug into the local history of the chapter and found it just as amazing. The chapter started in April 1964 when many of the campus leaders established Chi Sigma with the intention of becoming Sigma Chis. Paul Parets, a starry-eyed visionary, pledged a rival fraternity, but soon realized he made a mistake. He wanted true brotherhood, not just another place to party. With several friends they created a local. All they had to offer was a dream and passion. They soon found they were in good company.

Most of the original joiners and founders came from the honors dorm and were truly the movers and shakers on campus in those days. Included among them were the student body president, editor of the newspaper and some of the top athletes on campus.

Becoming Sigma Chi was their goal and they pursued it like a crusade. Chi Sigma became the Zeta Rho Chapter of Sigma Chi in 1967, a very short time for chartering in those days, but a testament to the tenacity of this group of individuals.

Sigma Chi landed at CMU in the spring of 1967 and went against the grain of every cultural trend. In the late '60s, the campus culturally went from Motown to "Helter Skelter." The spring and summer following their installation would see great urban riots and the assassinations of Robert F. Kennedy and Dr. Martin Luther King Jr. Needless to say, Sigma Chi's idealism seemed like an anachronism, but the chapter and its high ideals remain on campus today and it is the longest established fraternity in the school's history. In its first 50 years, more than 1,000 brothers joined.

The new chapter immediately won nearly every award the fraternity offers for scholarship, publications and public service, and it was honored as a Significant Chapter for many years. In 1970, Dave Wolds won the International Balfour Award given to the top undergraduate in the entire fraternity each year.

It was hard to explain to Greek Letter World non-believers and those who look down on fraternities that I was among the very best of the best and was damn proud of it. Being around leaders inspired me, and the semester I pledged I achieved the highest semester GPA of my college career.

When my initiation came, I was prepared and eager to make it official. I-Week, or Initiation Week, was an ordeal. We pretty much had to sequester ourselves all week, remain as silent as possible and study some pretty profound things. We had meetings each night of the week that featured heady discussions and self-examination. One of the unique things of our chapter was that before we began formal initiation, we were all initiated into our founding chapter Chi Sigma. It added immensely to the entire experience and connected us with our history.

As initiation ceremonies began there was a transition from "pledge" to "candidate." They called us one-by-one into a small, darkened room, lit by candlelight. We had to recite the Sigma Chi Creed, and other writings relevant to Sigma Chi.

Most of us choked at this exercise, but I recited it all perfectly. We were then asked to hand over our pledge pin, whereupon the pledge trainer looked at it, threw it to the ground and said sternly, *"You are no longer a pledge of this fraternity!"* It was at this point some of my pledge brothers lost it, thinking they had failed. Some of those brothers cried because they thought they were being dismissed. Not me! I was excited when I heard that. The trainer then stated, *"You are now a candidate for initiation!"* The only thought that ran through my head at that moment was *"Hot damn, pledging's over!"*

I can't share the details of the initiation, but it was an enlightening, highly emotional and cerebral event. It was full of history, heraldry and enduring fundamental human truths and principles. It was one of those life-changing experiences that only a prepared heart and mind can fully comprehend.

The friendships and connections I have with my fraternity brothers are enduring. A few years ago, my wife Kathy and I attended the Central Michigan-Purdue football game in West Lafayette, Indiana. I made connections with a CMU brother from an earlier time, Jim Vruggink, who was now the head of collegiate licensing at Purdue. Jim was my predecessor as Chapter Editor of the fraternity newsletter and a fellow journalism graduate. He won several publication awards from Sigma Chi when he was in the chapter.

Jim had been Purdue's sports information director and his mark is all over the Purdue campus. I first met Jim before I came to CMU; he was part of the M-Day my dad organized in Battle Creek for many years. He was in the sports information department at the University of Michigan not too long after graduating from CMU. He got the job partly through his connections with Sigma Chi. Will Perry, who was a Sigma Chi at Michigan, was the sports information director there and took a liking to Vruggink, who was a sports writer at the Ypsilanti Press. Vruggink later went on to become the sports information director at Northwestern University, once again through a Sigma Chi connection to the Northwestern football coach and later athletic director John Pont.

Vruggink employed my roommate, fellow journalism student and fraternity brother Gary Henderson, as a summer intern at Northwestern. Gary also summered at the Northwestern Sigma Chi house and had a memorable experience. He ended up in Washington as a press secretary for several congressmen before returning to Michigan where he became chief of staff for state senator

George McManus of Traverse City. A few years later Gary was the best man in my wedding.

Following the football game (CMU beat Purdue 38-17), Vruggink gave us a personal tour of the stadium, press box and other athletic facilities. The Ross-Ade Stadium is named for alumni David Ross and George Ade. Ade was a prominent cartoonist and Sigma Chi from Purdue who authored the Sigma Chi Creed. Jim organized the showcases to both men in the stadium lobby where Sigma Chi is prominently recognized in Ade's tribute. He later took us through Mackey Arena where he organized and collected memorabilia for the display cases paying tribute to Purdue's basketball coaches, athletes and legacies.

Purdue is home to one of the most legendary Sigma Chi chapters in the nation. The Delta Delta chapter has produced business leaders, athletes and astronauts. Vruggink also spearheaded the $5-million drive to restore the house, making it one of the grandest chapter houses in the nation.

I caught up with Vruggink and others from the past at our 50th Anniversary in 2017.

Paul Parets, the leader and founder who started it all, remarked that Sigma Chi is like a wall. From a distance, it looks sturdy and impenetrable. But as you get closer you notice that some of the bricks don't match. The mortar around some is giving out, and some of the bricks are chipped, cracked and damaged. Yet, he added, if we remove some, the wall weakens and collapses. This is how he described Sigma Chi: a collection of imperfect bricks, joined together on a strong foundation to create a solid wall. We were all awestruck by his words, more than 50 years after the foundation was built for Sigma Chi at CMU. His analogy is still dead accurate.

Joining the fraternity has given me great advantages in the larger Sigma Chi network because, over the years, the fraternity has attracted and created some of the very best leaders in all walks of life. My relationship with Sigma Chi has had a profound impact on my life, giving me much favor and distinction.

Lesson Learned

Among the things that attracted me to Sigma Chi were its rich history and traditions. I was also impressed with the quality and achievement of the alumni; Sigma Chi has many famous and outstanding leaders in the ranks. But what also impressed me was the quality and character of the local founders. Sigma Chi at CMU was created by a group of high achievers who had big dreams and big ideals. I would be joining a legacy of true leaders and visionaries. No other fraternity on campus could offer that or even come close. Most were just social clubs.

In April 2017, the Zeta Rho Chapter celebrated its 50th anniversary on campus, and is now the longest-standing continuous organization there. I was involved with the Golden event and rubbed shoulders with the original Chi Sigmas (the founding local). It was a spiritual weekend, to say the least.

Sigma Chi and most other fraternities today **Defy the Immediate**, as they've done for most of their existence. Fraternities are mysterious organizations to those who don't understand them, and today they face much persecution in politically correct academia. A few acts of stupidity and hazing, which shouldn't happen or be tolerated, have ruined it for Greeks on many campuses.

Fraternities remain institutions that can enhance academic achievement and build great citizens. For many, they offer the first taste of real leadership, teamwork and conflict resolution, and dealing with group dynamics. Fraternities often get a bad rap today, but they endure as one of our nation's great character-producing institutions.

CHAPTER 7

Anchors Aweigh

"A good Navy is not a provocation to war. It is the surest guaranty of peace!"

— Theodore Roosevelt

After graduating from Central Michigan University in the spring of 1982, I received my orders to Navy Officer Candidate School in Newport, Rhode Island, reporting in September. With a job secured, it was time to have some fun.

One of the highlights of that summer was caravanning to Flathead Lake, Montana, with Joe Schwarz and his family. I followed him across the country in my '73 Chevy Impala and helped him move many items out to the family's retreat.

At that time, the Schwarz family was Joe, his wife, Anne, who grew up in Kalispell and the Flathead Valley, their daughter, Brennan, Joe's elderly mother, Helen, a WWI Army nurse, and Arnie the Wonder Dog.

They loaded up their Pontiac station wagon with a huge carrier on top so Brennan would have a play area in the back. My trunk and back seat were packed full of many things Joe needed in Montana, including a prized original painting by renowned Montana artist Charlie Russell. One of Joe's lifelong ambitions was to own an original Charlie Russell and he finally got one. It still graces that Montana home.

I also had an extended member of their family as my co-pilot.

Joe had a mutual friend and physician in Japan who wanted his son to attend school in the United States. Joe and Anne took Youske Maki into their home while he attended high school. That summer was Youske's first year in the U.S. and he hadn't mastered English. It was a challenge communicating with him. Fortunately my car had a top-of-the-line Pioneer stereo and we had plenty of cassette tapes for the entire trip. Youske had an affinity for Olivia Newton-John and we rocked with her across the U.S.A.

When I drove home to Michigan by myself, Olivia never made it to the tape deck.

We had a great time and spent many days in Glacier National Park and just hanging out on Flathead Lake. I loved seeing Joe in a setting where he could relax and open up. We had many heady discussions on different subjects and he was truly a mentor. We discussed issues of the day, the military and some of the things I'd be getting into. Occasionally, Anne piped in, too. They had met as CIA operatives in Jakarta, Indonesia.

It wasn't long after that trip that Anne was diagnosed with breast cancer and began treatment. A few years later, the cancer took her life. After the diagnosis, she spent as much time in her beloved Montana as she could.

After spending my last leisurely summer days at Gull Lake, September came and it was time to shove off for a new adventure and career in the U.S. Navy.

I loaded up my Impala and headed east, spending a few days sightseeing along the way. The night before I reported, I stayed in a historic hotel in Old Saybrook, Connecticut.

The next day I checked out Newport. I figured that things would soon get intense, and that I should enjoy it while I could. Newport is a seaport community and home to the America's Cup, the crown jewel of the sailing world. The Cup had been in Newport for more than 100 years. I fell in love with Newport's charm and history and spent much of my liberty time exploring it.

I arrived at the main gate and was directed to the Navy base administration building when I pulled in the next morning. I stepped out of the car and it hit me like a freight train. The ocean salt smell blown by a bay breeze was almost overwhelming. I took in a deep breath of that salty air. It smelled new, fresh and full of opportunity. This was the right decision for me, I thought, anxious for what would come next.

Lesson Learned

Some people back home thought I was crazy for joining the military. I saw it as the next big thing in my life. *It's not just a job, it's an adventure* as the recruiting posters say, and they certainly delivered! Over the next four months I would be tested and challenged in ways I couldn't imagine.

I took full advantage of my last free summer. I knew my life was about to take a dramatic turn. My time in Montana gave me much to think about and to reflect on where I'd been and where I was going.

When I crossed the quarterdeck at King Hall in Newport, I again was a freshman, so to speak, and had to learn a new way of life. It was exciting and each day presented opportunities to **Defy the Immediate.**

OCS would become one of the best times in my military career. After weeks of hard work and learning, we would proudly put on the gold bar of Ensign in the U.S. Navy. I looked forward to being a player on a huge world stage. It was an opportunity few get to realize and one that we didn't take for granted. I considered myself fortunate, so to speak.

CHAPTER 8

Cage Those Eyes!

"A great attitude does much more than turn on the lights in our worlds; it seems to magically connect us to all sorts of serendipitous opportunities that were somehow absent before the change."

— Earl Nightingale

After arriving at Naval Station Newport, Rhode Island, to report aboard Officer Candidate School, a few of us took our bags and headed to the quarterdeck at King Hall. We were promptly greeted by a senior officer candidate.

The class always has two groups, a junior and senior class. The new seniors became seniors a day earlier when the class ahead of them graduated. We were the new junior class. You'd think the new seniors had become admirals with their newfound sense of authority. This will be fun, I thought.

We were told to put our bags on the sidewalk and line up. Most of us had little or no military experience. We didn't know how to come to attention. We were told to stand straight and look ahead. When someone started looking around, the pseudo drill instructor shouted *Cage those eyes!* We had no idea what they were talking about and we laughed about it later as we made a cage over our eyes with our fingers.

They screamed and hollered at us and we missed most of the things they said. You almost wanted to reply, *"You don't have to shout!"*

They kept talking about the SWARM. Everything we needed to know was in the SWARM. But we were clueless what the SWARM was, as the acronyms and new vocabulary came fast and furious.

I was assigned to OSCAR Company and I got to my room on the fourth deck (we didn't call them floors in the Navy). The fourth deck was the top of the building – we had the penthouse! That was good because it was easy to keep clean since we were the only ones using it. It was quiet and had a beautiful view of Narragansett Bay. Part of our daily routine was cleaning our areas before inspection at lights out each night. We had an ongoing war with knurdles, or dustballs. We would be docked precious points if the inspector found knurdles. It was perhaps the cleanest placed I ever lived in!

The other decks were traversed by everyone and were hard to keep clean. The trade-off for the penthouse was that we had to climb four flights of stairs (or ladders) several times every day.

When I got settled in my two-man room, my roommate, Gene Mincey, who became a supply officer, and I tried to figure out what was going on. We both shrugged and agreed they'd let us know soon enough.

There were a few books and publications on the desk that we would use. Among them was the *Standard Organization and Regulation Manual*, the SORM (not SWARM) they were talking about. The SORM had everything you needed to know about OCS and it behooved you to know it forward and backward. It answered many of our questions.

I quickly learned that the military has a whole new language and when you hear an acronym, you need to know, or find out, what it means.

We all settled into the routine of OCS. The first week was a challenge, but it's supposed to be. It's meant to be a transition from civilian to military life. You get shouted at, ridiculed and, still, it's not so bad. At the end of I-Week we felt a sense of accomplishment that we'd made it through the hardest part of OCS. Following that, it was more like an intense college class.

The routine was well organized, but you covered about 25 subjects in 16 weeks. You had to concentrate and study hard at night to keep up because everything was new. I actually enjoyed the physical training we did as a relief from the classroom.

While I grasped most subjects easily, math – as it has been all my life – remained my challenge. In those days we learned celestial navigation and had to calculate our location based on the position of the stars and the sun. It's really just math problems, but you've got to do everything correctly. You do the math from the time of day and figures in the publications. When you get your answer, you verify it by looking at and measuring the star or the sun. If you are correct, you plot it on a chart. You have to do three calculations of bodies at different angles and when you plot them, the three lines should intersect on the chart to give you your position. The smaller the triangle of the three lines intersecting, the more accurate the plot.

Celestial navigation is a mostly lost art in today's world of GPS and satellite technology, but it requires correct calculations. Fortunately, I worked hard to understand it and nailed it on my final exam.

I also struggled with the maneuvering board. MOBoard, as it's called, is a paper compass plot about the size of a pizza board that is used to plot radar information and allows you to figure out another ship's course and speed after plotting several radar pings. The most important thing you calculated was the other ships' CPA or Closest Point of Approach. You had to know in advance whether to alter your course if the ship might pass too close or cross your bow at a short range. It took me some time to perform the calculations since it required both math and geometry. When it became obvious I was having challenges passing the first few quizzes, one of the instructors came to my aid.

While at OCS I learned about a different kind of officer, the LDO or Limited Duty Officer. LDOs are superstar enlisted sailors who are given an officer commission but are restricted to duty only in their field of expertise. For example, an Ordnanceman LDO could only work in a weapons department and an Engineman LDO could only work in engineering. They are restricted line officers and not eligible for command. Often they are called Mustangs.

Fortunately, one of the best Quartermaster (experts in navigation) sailors who became LDO was an instructor at OCS. He saw my struggles and offered to tutor me over lunch. I met him in his office and he brought in a couple of McDonald's Quarter Pounders since we were both missing lunch. It had been a few weeks since I'd seen fast food. What a treat!

Over the lunch hour this LDO lieutenant explained how MoBoard worked and we did a few problems using a radar scenario. Before long, it clicked. If he had not taken the time and interest in me, I probably would have flunked the course and might have been rolled back to the next class. You only get to "roll back" once. After that you go to a board and face possible discharge. One of the sayings around OCS was *"Don't sweat it. Nimitz was a rollback!"* That wasn't very good advice!

Once I got to the fleet, MoBoard was second nature and I could look out the window and see that my calculation was correct by the way the ship was moving. Before long, I could see movement and calculate rate, time and distance in my head. Geometry is simple when it's real. My problem with math was when it was conceptual. When I saw it applied, it made sense.

A few weeks into OCS we realized that after 1700, or 5 p.m., we were on our own with no authority figures around. Sure, there were watch officers, but they were all our classmates. We were college grads and eventually pushed the limits on what we could get away with. Evenings became social events, especially in our senior semester.

Each night, about a half hour before "Taps," one of our classmates designated as the Officer Candidate Fleet Admiral (OCFAD) would don his apparel – PT (physical training) gear with swim fins, a goofy admiral's hat and huge admiral shoulder boards, plus a duck's beak. As the OCFAD descended from the fourth deck, all the candidates on lower decks would come to attention as the first one to notice him shouted: "Attention on Duck!" When the OCFAD got to the first deck he would go into the courtyard, often with trumpet and flourishes. He would then do the daily countdown, which was something like *"22 days left at OCS; 15 more exams; 8 more liberty calls,"* etc., etc. He would end with, *"That is all, carry on!"*

It was a tradition we looked forward to; the OCFAD would often mention funny things that happened or call out someone who did something stupid. It was a morale booster and a fond memory from an intense time.

At liberty in Newport, we could break free of the school and hit several bars and taverns. The Brick Alley Pub was one of our favorites. On free weekends we toured the mansions and learned about Newport's history.

After eight weeks, our class graduated and we became the new seniors and were granted more freedom; we had Wednesday night and most of the weekend free. When we were being trained, many of the ships still had WWII-era boilers and we learned about maintaining their propulsion boilers. We learned two cleaning techniques. The first was known as "surface blow," a routine cleaning of the water and sediment on the top. The second was more extensive and required a complete draining of the boiler and a "bottom blow" to remove all sediment.

One of the more colorful candidates in our company dubbed Wednesday night liberty as "surface blow" and weekend liberty as "bottom blow." Obviously there was some sexual innuendo as someone would ask, *"So where are we going for surface blow tonight?"* Ah, the crusty language of sailors!

One of the treats at OCS was Chief Warrant Officer 4 Wally Exum, an instructor who was a chief petty officer at Pearl Harbor on Dec. 7, 1941, the day of the Japanese attack on the Navy's Pacific fleet. He was aboard the battleship USS Nevada, the only ship to get safely underway before the attack. He authored the book "Battleship!" and taught the Navy's history. His stories of Pearl Harbor were gripping and he often got emotional during class. He retired shortly after I graduated from OCS.

In the last two weeks of OCS we prepared for our assignments to the fleet, becoming an ensign and going on to a career. One of the great pre-commissioning events is billet selection night where we choose, sort of, our first duty assignment. All the billets or jobs in the fleet are posted on a wall and grouped by your specialty. Most candidates, like me, were on the traditional Surface Warfare Officer track, and most of the billets were division officer jobs on surface ships. All the supply officer candidates go to Athens, Georgia, for Supply School and the nuclear candidates go to Surface Nuclear Reactor School in Idaho, so they didn't participate. In all, about 100 of us would earn our "butter bars" at graduation and go on to our next school before joining the fleet.

Like everything else in the military, there is a pecking order and at OCS you choose your billet, or assignment by class standing. At that time, the Navy was bringing back the battleships and there were many junior officer billets on the USS New Jersey, Iowa, Missouri and Wisconsin. All of them were grabbed quickly by the students in the top of the class. Following those, the new Spruance class destroyers, cruisers and older destroyers and then frigates, amphibious and auxiliary ships went quickly and pretty much in that order.

Unfortunately, my class standing was awful – second to last – when the listing came out. Although I felt good about my academic work at OCS and achieved a decent GPA in a competitive environment, I was lucky to graduate with my class and rejoiced I didn't become a rollback and have to repeat another 16 weeks as some in my class did.

One of the things someone said to me was that your gold bar at commissioning will be identical to everyone else's, so don't sweat it. True, but not good advice at the moment. The better candidates got the better jobs!

My turn came at the very end of billet selection night. By the time I made it into the room for my selection, I had just two choices: a tugboat in Bahrain or the aircraft carrier USS Nimitz (CVN 68). No smart junior surface officer would voluntarily take a billet on a carrier. It's an aviation platform, run by aviators, a different breed of officer. I'd heard horror stories about being a junior officer on a carrier. Getting surface warfare-qualified there would be a challenge.

But after thinking about it briefly, I grabbed the Nimitz billet. I figured carrier life would be more interesting than being on a tiny ship in a Middle East port. Who knows how different my career and life would have been had I taken the tugboat. I was likely needed there and would have been part of a small, elite team. Much of life is based on your choices of the moment. Did I choose the right job? I'll never know, but the next four years in the fleet would be exciting and I looked forward to being on a highly visible platform.

When graduation came, my parents, sister and, unexpectedly, Harriet Lindauer, a close family friend, drove out for the commissioning and graduation ceremony. Harriet always thought of me as a son and I was delighted to have her.

At graduation, I was commissioned an Ensign – one of the proudest moments of my life. It was a goal I set out to achieve and I had made it! I had defied the immediate and truly accomplished something. I was ready to take on the world!

After a well-earned leave, I returned to Newport to attend Surface Warfare Officer School (SWOS) where you learn the real nuts and bolts of being a junior officer in the fleet. I couldn't wait!

Lesson Learned

Getting through Officer Candidate School was a struggle! In many ways I was out of my league, competing with others with technical backgrounds or who already had Navy experience in the fleet. Many times I feared I wouldn't make it, but I learned there are generous people willing to help. This is true in any endeavor in life. You just have to find them and trust them!

I was fortunate I was in a program where the goal was to get people to succeed. OCS is creating future officers and there were talented people to get you to that goal, but you had to work for it. If you are willing to work hard, stay motivated, do what's needed, and then a little extra, your effort is rewarded.

I had **Defied the Immediate** and reached my goal of becoming a naval officer.

Graduation was one of my proudest moments. I was a commissioned officer in the United States Navy!

CHAPTER 9

America's Cup Beckons

"If one does not know to which port one is sailing, no wind is favorable."
                                        — Lucius Annaeus Seneca

If it wasn't difficult enough getting through OCS, Surface Warfare Officer School (SWOS), my next step in Newport before going to the fleet, would be every bit as challenging.

Many of my classmates returned to settle into the school. As commissioned officers we were no longer bound by the rules and schedule of OCS. We were now 9-5 students with freedom.

I began SWOS in the spring of 1983. It was the summer that got me in trouble. As luck would have it, 1983 was an America's Cup summer, the last for Newport, and the town turned into a big party every night.

Each of the contenders — the Americans, the Brits, the Aussies and the Italians — had their own haunts. The party and bar scene became a distraction from my studies in SWOS and earned me an academic board after bombing a few tests. Most of the senior officers in charge understood the distraction and let me off with a warning, but I was under the gun to finish SWOS.

One of the huge America's Cup stories was the Australian boat, which ultimately took the cup from Newport after a century of competition. Their new super-secret keel was the story of the year in yachting. The Aussies went to great lengths to hide the keel from the media. The boat was more secure than the Navy base. They frequently had to fend off nosy divers and it was rumored that Navy SEALS were covertly guarding it. It was a media spectacle. I had an opportunity to spend a thrilling day on a spectator boat watching the race up close. The boats were fast and competitive.

I was starting to fall behind in my studies at SWOS and had to bear down. I gave up a few weekends to study and get decent grades and avoid academic failure.

One scary moment came when I failed a critical test. I was taken to an academic board with the SWOS commanding officer and had to account for it.

I was honest and said I spent too much time downtown and along the waterfront and didn't study as hard as I should have. He and the department heads agreed that America's Cup was a huge distraction, but they laid it on the line: If I failed another test I risked being expelled from the school. After the frank ass-chewing, they voted to keep me in the program. I was never sure if it was just a way to scare me, but it worked!

I made the extra effort, got through everything and graduated with my class on time once again. I was ready to move to my first assignment.

While at SWOS, my orders arrived and I was surprised to see I was going to the USS Dwight D. Eisenhower (CVN 69). It didn't matter, but I was surprised I hadn't been assigned to the Nimitz.

I now had to go to sea and prove myself to earn my surface warfare pin. I was ready for the challenge!

On my first cruise in the Mediterranean, we had a port call in Trieste, Italy. The Yacht Club at Trieste was home to the Italian America's Cup contender Azzura. The officer's landing was at the yacht club and the club opened all its facilities to our officers. We had a chance to have a true international experience.

Lesson Learned

After graduating from OCS, Surface Warfare School seemed more laidback, and it was. But you can't rest on your laurels in the military. I worked hard, but also took advantage of the freedom and status I had as a new officer. I enjoyed Newport too much during the America's Cup summer and it hurt my performance in class. I had to be shocked into working harder and sat through a humiliating board to remember what my mission was, learning the craft of surface warfare.

Simply put, I had to **Defy the Immediate**, which was a nightly party with people from all over the world. As a Navy officer, we had clout in town and could do things and go places others couldn't. I don't regret the experience of that America's Cup summer, but I had to learn to prioritize my time and keep my goals in perspective. I learned the lesson in time management and focusing the hard way.

Life requires priorities and perseverance, but don't forget to have fun along the way!

CHAPTER 10

Carrier Landing – I Like IKE!

"One of the greatest discoveries a man makes, one of his great surprises, is to find he can do what he was afraid he couldn't do."

— Henry Ford

After a year in Newport with OCS and SWOS, it was time to get to the fleet. I took a few weeks of leave in Michigan before loading up the Impala and heading to Norfolk to catch a flight that would take me on a 36-hour odyssey to Bagel Station, off the coast of Lebanon in the eastern Mediterranean.

One of the things we learned in training was "getting the gouge." Gouge is a Navy term for advice. You don't ask for advice – you "get the gouge." Gouge isn't always correct or accurate.

Anyway, I asked around about what uniform to wear while traveling to the carrier. Someone suggested that to make the best first impression I should wear my summer whites. Very bad gouge! They were trashed by the time I reached the ship.

I boarded a commercial plane in Norfolk to get to Philadelphia. In Philly, we switched to a Military Airlift Command (MAC) flight. It's like a commercial jet without flight attendants, soft drinks or peanuts.

I didn't know how to make the transition from commercial to MAC, so I asked questions such as "Will my bags transfer?" They don't. You have to get them and check them in yourself. Whoops, I didn't. Fortunately, some of the flight crew who knew about junior officers in this situation bailed me out. The bags stayed with me for the rest of the trip.

We flew over the Atlantic and made a brief stop in the Azores, where it was night, to pick up a few more passengers. As I looked out the window, I could see hundreds of rabbits scurrying off the runway when we lifted off. It was still dark when we landed late in Sigonella, Sicily. We were supposed to board the carrier-based C-2 Greyhound cargo aircraft, but it wasn't going to take off until daylight. Those of us still at the airport had to stick around in case they decided to leave early. Some people slept but I couldn't. This is where I first heard the

The author was a young ensign on his first shipboard assignment when this photo, with Yeoman Kenny Baldwin, was taken aboard the USS Dwight D. Eisenhower. Shaw was an administrative assistant in the weapons department.

term "mill about smartly" when I asked what we should do. I sat and read, chatted with people and just waited to get on the flight.

At daybreak, we grabbed our gear and headed to the C-2. The flight team loaded our luggage and briefed us before we walked up the ramp. We donned inflatable life jackets, headsets and helmets and, one by one, crawled into the back of the aircraft, which holds about 12. We faced backward and strapped ourselves into the nylon jump seats. Before takeoff, a young aircrewman came by, checked our seatbelts, and gave them seemingly sadistic tugs to make certain we were well secured. An aircrewman closed the ramp and the only light in the hold was from small portholes. Once the plane was airborne, the aircrewman pulled out a sleeping bag and went to sleep. As we took off, I got as comfortable as I could and fell asleep with the drone of the engines for the four-hour flight across the Mediterranean.

As we neared the carrier, the aircrewman made sure we were awake and re-briefed us on our positions for landing. When he gave the signal, we were to cross our arms over our chests and lean into the seat belts. It seemed like an eternity leaning forward in anticipation of the landing, often described as a controlled crash.

Our position in the cargo hold was a few feet from the tail hook. Even with headsets on, it sounds like you're crashing when the tail hook hits the deck. To be honest, it scared the daylights out of me. Since you are leaning into straps and you are facing backward and in the dark, you don't know what's happened. All of a sudden you are at a dead stop and you start breathing again.

The plane taxied for a minute, the engines shut down and the ramp opened to a sunny and hot Mediterranean day at sea. I stepped onto the deck of the USS Dwight D. Eisenhower, the only one on the plane in whites, and was escorted to the Air Terminal Office for check-in.

After being corralled into the Air Terminal Office (ATO), I was met by John Severino, a lieutenant junior grade. He was eager to see me as I was his relief in the Weapons Department. Sev, a Naval Academy graduate, was the weapons administrative assistant, or the WAA as the junior officer billet was known. The job was supervising two yeomen and a personnel man in the department office. Also in the office was the ship's weapons officer, a very senior commander aviator who oversaw a department of about 300 aviation ordnance-men and gunnersmates, the redshirts on the flight deck. These were the guys who handled and moved the bombs and missiles and loaded and unloaded the planes, sometimes on a daily basis. They also maintained the armories and the ship's small arms and handled some of the more sophisticated weapons and systems on the ship.

Before I could settle in and get my room, Severino took me to see the executive officer, Capt. Dayton Ritt. I was so tired, I just wanted to get it over with. Still in my trashed whites I was not so sure I made a good impression. I got the customary "welcome aboard" chat and don't remember much.

Finally, I arrived in the supply department to get my stateroom assignment. Unfortunately, they didn't get word I was coming, so they put me up temporarily in a room with mid-grade officers. It was a two-man room where the occupant, a lieutenant commander from the Operations Department (Ops Dept.), was on leave. The room was nice, quiet, and cool below the hangar deck and I think I slept for about 15 hours. I finally met the roommate, another 0-4 from the Ops Department, who helped me find the wardroom for some food. I was starving, totally lost on the ship and completely unfamiliar with the routine.

Days later, I got a four-man room in junior officer quarters. My roommate was a fellow officer from OCS, Ensign Dennis Ward, who had also recently joined the ship. We ended up working together to get our qualifications. The other berths were assigned to two tech reps, civilians from the Grumman Aerospace aircraft company, or "Grummies" as we called them. They were paid well to go to sea and order parts for the aircraft and be available to the squadrons. They were a blast on liberty because they had no restrictions or duty and were our rides because they could rent cars in port. You could rent a car if you were senior enough and didn't care about rules. I found in the Navy that rules, regulations and laws had big differences.

Our room was under the jet blast deflector (JBD) and next to the machinery room for the catapult retract motor. It shook during flight operations and I came to discern the differences in sound between a booming F-14 and a relatively quiet S-3 when they launched. Can you imagine an F-14 on your roof? We also heard every piece of yellow gear (the tractors that move planes around) and tie-down chains being dragged and dropped on the deck.

It became a symphony of predicable sounds during flight ops. You could hear the JBD go up, then hear the afterburners ignite, kick in and roar for about 30 seconds. There was a clunk when they released the brake and you could hear the roar go off in the distance as the catapult shuttle (where the plane attaches to the catapult) hits the end of the deck with another metallic thump. It was eerily quiet for about 15 seconds, then the retract motor kicked in, bringing the shoe back for the next plane with an annoying whine. Then the process started over. It was amazing that you could learn to sleep through it.

After getting settled in and learning my way around the ship, I began my job in the weapons department. They give you these jobs, which are pretty simple, because your real goal there is operational and to stand watch and get qualified. The weapons administrative assistant was a typically easy junior officer job, but my department head, an aviation commander whose flying days were over, found ways to make it difficult. He was close to retirement, so mentoring a junior officer wasn't high on his priority list. I spent as little time as I could in the office and preferred to be out and about getting to know people on the decks and who was who in the department. I found the weapons department had many limited duty officers (LDOs) and warrant officers, many of whom were now senior and had spent hard time in Vietnam. Some were excellent; others seemed jaded. The most senior LDO in the department (and on the ship) was a lieutenant commander named Mike Cain, who was the ordnance handling officer, or the OHO.

The OHO is in charge of all the weapons movements on the ship and doesn't mess around. I discovered that Cain had been anointed the King of the LDOs on the ship. He had his own table in the ward room at meal time and most of the other LDOs flocked around him. He was a straight shooter. He liked to tell ensigns he had held every rank in the Navy – except ensign! I learned a lot from him. He regularly dispensed advice and opinions on everything and bragged about how much leave time he had accumulated because he had spent so much time at sea. On his stateroom door was a bumper sticker that read "LDO for CNO!" (Chief of Navy Operations). He eventually retired as a captain, a great achievement for an LDO.

I was still new, and never had been to a foreign port in the Navy. I was looking forward to it. We were scheduled to visit Alexandria, Egypt, and as the new admin officer in the Weapons Department, I attended a port call planning meeting. At this meeting, we went over which department was responsible for what during the visit. Costs for port visits include things like harbor pilot services, utilities, pier rent, security, tariffs and more. The cost is divided among each department's OPTAR (Operational Target) budget. The Executive Officer (XO) handed out instructions detailing the responsibilities of each department. Weapons would provide funding for the camels. I did a double take.

I had forgotten that in the Navy "camels" were the floating barges that go between the ship and the pier, sort of like the rubber fenders you throw over the side of your boat so you don't bump the dock. Often these camels have a tank to handle oily discharge from the ship to keep the harbor clean. Navy vocabulary still challenged me.

I asked: *"What are we doing with camels?"* (Thinking of the mammal, not the barge). An astute senior officer noticed my ignorance and stated, *"Shore patrol. Camels are the best mode of transportation over here."* "You're kidding, right?" I asked. No, he said, *"We're going to have a corral on the pier and you're going to be in charge of feeding and watering them!"* Everyone (except me) laughed. I was still puzzled, but knew I had been pimped. I shut up and later found out what the camels were. Geez, did I feel stupid. I was living up to the reputation of an ensign.

The port call to Egypt was ultimately canceled as the captain, in discussion with the medical officer, determined that the conditions there would likely pose a health risk. He didn't want to risk knocking out part of the crew who might catch something there after an extended time at sea. Still, I would have loved to have seen Egypt.

We changed directions and headed west across the Mediterranean for Naples, Italy, where I would get my first port visit.

I went to the bridge as we passed through the Strait of Messina, the narrow passage between mainland Italy and Sicily, the toe and the football! It's a congested crossing with hundreds of boats and ferries. We had to post special watches for this because many boats passed extremely close to the ship, many out of sight of the bridge. It made for a nerve-wracking hour. We couldn't count on other boats to follow the usual rules of the road. Instead, we relied more on the Law of Gross Tonnage – we were huge and unable to stop quickly so smaller vessels needed to yield to us.

Once we reached Naples, we dropped anchor – another huge operation. Each anchor weighs about 30,000 pounds and when one drops, the entire front end of the ship rattles as anchor chain pays out.

Once the ship was safely moored and watch was set, the much-anticipated liberty call commenced and sailors flooded the Naples port in search of liquor and beer. We had been at sea for 96 days straight before this port call; the crew was ready to party.

Before going on liberty, the Supply Department set up a station on the mess deck to exchange currency. Typically, we would take $100 or so and exchange it for lira, pesos, drachma or whatever the local denomination was. It prevented many sailors from getting ripped off in town. This was long before the euro. A few years ago, I found my box of foreign money. It took me awhile, but after separating all the bills and coins I think I had about $700.

At Fleet Landing, hundreds of vendors had stands along the street. They are known to the fleet as "Hey Joe's" because they all shout "Hey Joe!" in broken Italian as sailors pass. The vendors offer clothing, souvenirs, "fine" jewelry and even pornography. It's almost impossible to walk past without getting harassed. You try to avoid eye contact. Some reputable vendors were screened and invited to set up on the mess deck during port calls. If they were on the ship, it was safe to buy from them. One, Silvio Polidoro, was a good tailor and frequent visitor. People raved about his custom clothing. I bought a really nice wool suit from him. I still have it today. He even sewed my name on the inside pocket.

I got ashore for a day and wandered around Naples. A bus was available for rides to the NATO base, and on the first night several of us dined at the Allied Officers Club there. I couldn't believe it; a dinner roll fight broke out among many of the aviators. Apparently it's a tradition, so we started picking up rolls and throwing them back. When in Rome (or Naples!) We were warned about walking just outside the base and to be aware of the "Ricciones." They looked like women, but they weren't!

On the second day in port, I stood at anchor watch on the quarter deck as Officer of the Deck Under Instruction, OODUI. My job was to observe what happened and supervise the comings and goings of personnel. It was also the communication center and you had control over the ship's systems, bells, whistles and gongs.

I'll never forget what happened on that first watch.

About the time we set anchor, we heard that something bad had happened to the Marines in Beirut. Initial reports were sketchy, but we heard there was an attack.

When the carrier was patrolling the gun line off Beirut for several months, our aircraft created detailed maps of the area and who was where. The F-14 jets aboard the carrier employed TARPS (Tactical Air Reconnaissance Photo System), which literally created strip maps for intelligence gathering on a daily basis.

Who would launch an attack and how? We later learned it was the first volley in the new form of warfare called terrorism. We were dumbfounded that a suicide truck drove into the Marine barracks in Beirut, killing 241 U.S. servicemen, 58 French soldiers, six civilians and both suicide bombers.

During that first quarterdeck watch at anchor in Naples Harbor, Capt. Ritt came down and told us to end liberty and begin recall procedures. We were leaving. Shore patrol started rounding everyone up. One of the signs of a recall was that the ship's helicopter, an H-3, flies over with its dipping sonar down. This is a signal to get back to the ship. It's very effective.

Everyone came rushing back, knowing something had happened in Beirut. The liberty boats were operating one way now and rounding up the crew. Shortly after recall began, we shifted the watch from the quarterdeck to the bridge. Ritt was getting the ship underway in the absence of the commanding officer, Capt. Ed Clexton, who was in Rome on official business. The ship's helicopter flew up to get him. We pushed off with only a few people left ashore, which was remarkable.

Within four hours IKE was headed to Bagel Station. Just as the ship began leaving the Naples harbor, the H-3 helicopter with Clexton aboard landed and he took command. We went back through the Strait of Messina at an unusually high speed, bordering on dangerous, and headed east.

During my time in the Navy, that transit back to Bagel Station was the only time I really experienced war nerves. As the pieces of the puzzle unraveled about what had happened in Beirut, we grew angry. Everyone on the ship, despite a shortened liberty, came together. Ordnance moved to the flight deck at a feverish pace and the redshirts quickly loaded the aircraft.

We expected to launch a retaliatory attack. Loaded and piloted F-14s sat on the catapults for hours, waiting for word to launch as we sailed back to the gunline. I remember looking down from the bridge at night and seeing a Tomcat pilot sitting at his controls reading a novel while his RIO (Radar Intercept Officer) sat behind him snoozing with the canopy open on a breezy Mediterranean evening. There was an eager anticipation do to something, something swift and decisive. But we didn't.

The executive officer of the Marine detachment, Capt. Josh Bocchino, tried desperately to go ashore in Beirut and help his fellow Marines. But he wasn't allowed to leave the ship. He was frustrated.

We later came to understand that an aircraft carrier and a carrier strike group, with all its firepower, was useless against this brand of primitive warfare. How does a carrier task force defend against a truck bomb? We're still trying to figure it out today.

We spent a few weeks back at Bagel Station, continuing flight operations over Lebanon without any aggression. The Ordnancemen (Ordies) went through a continuous and frustrating cycle of loading and unloading planes for a few more weeks.

One day the USS Independence (CV 62) came over the horizon as our relief. What a beautiful sight!

After a few days of turnover and exchanges, we were westbound again and heading to Norfolk and home, sweet home, after one of IKE's longest and most demanding cruises. I came aboard toward the end of it, but I looked forward to more time underway. A carrier never stays in port long. I'd have many more chances to prove my mettle. I was still considered new at the end of this cruise.

In the days just after leaving the U.S. and coming back in, we loaded and unloaded all our ordnance just after all the aircraft joined or left the carrier. We had little to no ordnance and no aircraft aboard when we were in home port in Norfolk.

The day we offloaded from our first deployment, I stood as a safety observer on the hangar deck. We were off the Virginia Capes, eager to get home. For most of a day all the ordnance came up from the magazine and armory and was transferred to an ammunition ship by helicopters. The ship then took it to the Yorktown Weapons Station for storage. The OHO gave us cards that cross referenced all the bombs and missiles with beer brands for radio security. We were still in international waters and a Russian AGI or intelligence ship was nearby, monitoring our activity. You'd hear over your radio, "*Two pallets of Budweiser coming up!*" or "*The Molson is secured and ready for transfer!*"

The offload came after a brief time at sea, at least for me. When I arrived on IKE the carrier was at the end of one of its longest times ever at sea. I arrived during the last few weeks of what would be a 96-day stay on Bagel Station. It was also the last phase of the deployment. The crew had operationally forfeited at least two port visits and was ready for liberty ashore at home.

After some time back at homeport, IKE got underway for workups and another cruise.

It took some time before I was getting underway bridge watches, but eventually I rotated through with all the other junior officers. Before I got on the bridge, I spent lots of time crawling around the engineering spaces and learning how a nuclear-powered vessel worked. Reactor and engineering departments are separate, but together they ran the ship.

The people in the reactor department are highly specialized and trained. Many of the officers had gone through nuclear power school and had seniority. Being the reactor officer on a carrier is the pinnacle of a nuclear engineer's career. Many junior officers begin their nuclear careers fresh from nuke school. It seemed that new officers were coming on all the time. On many occasions a new nuclear ensign would show up in the wardroom and someone would remark, *"Looks like they're cloning new ensigns down there again!"*

Many of the nukes and engineers were surface warfare officers so they were great about helping junior shipboard officers like me with getting our qualifications. We were "black shoes on a brown shoe ship." Traditionally, line officers (ship drivers) wear black shoes and aviators wear brown shoes. The carrier, an aviation platform, is run by and commanded at nearly every level by aviators. Surface guys are also in operations and engineering, but are grossly outnumbered. That's why it's so difficult for a very junior surface officer to get ahead on an aviation platform.

In my opinion, aviators were better leaders. Those who have flown aircraft, landed on carriers and seen air-to-air combat know what's important and what's not. They've had close calls, fought hard for their qualifications and put in the hours, tricky landings and sweat equity to get ahead. While we all share comradery as naval officers, aviators have developed a heightened sense of confidence needed to perform their missions. They are often seen as arrogant by surface types, but after being around them, it was clear to me that they had earned the right to be a little cocky. When I became a public affairs officer, I invested in brown shoes and always wore them with my khakis. I identified more with aviators and it helped me in my public affairs career.

They are warriors.

The chasm between surface and aviation officers was sometimes subtle and sometimes pronounced. I remember when a gung-ho chief in the reactor department, a devoted surface type, did his training presentation on how the reactor works for the new officers and sailors. He couldn't help but take a jab at "Airdales" by saying the real mission of the aircraft and pilots is to simply provide the first line of damage control for the ship. It was interesting that the title of his presentation was "Zoomies and Nukes."

One aviator I stood watch with observed how surface guys worry about everything, and it's true. He put it in perspective. He observed that surface guys light off the "sweat pumps" and nearly go to general quarters (or high alert level) when a ship was going to pass just outside of 2,000 yards at 8 knots relative speed. He chuckled that aviators deal with planes flying a few feet from each other at 200 knots. He said, *"I can't believe you guys worry about a ship passing a mile from us in 20 minutes!"*

It's also interesting that while there is a rivalry between surface and air types, there is a great rivalry between specific aviators. The pecking order begins with lowly helicopter pilots (who you hope to see quickly when you eject), then advances to the E-2C guys (they actually run the mission in the air), then goes up to the attack and fighter types with the jet jockeys or "Top Guns" flying the

The crew of the USS Dwight D. Eisenhower spelled out IKE for a photo in the English Channel as President Ronald Reagan flew overhead in June 1984. Reagan was enroute to ceremonies in Normandy, France, marking the 40th anniversary of D-Day. The crew, including the author, hoped the president would land and visit with them, but his schedule didn't permit it. (U.S. Navy photo)

F-14s and now F/A 18s off the flight deck. All of them pick on each other like big and little brothers, but all of them seem to laugh at surface guys.

Aviators say the surface Navy *"eats their young,"* and after all my experiences I can't disagree with that analysis. As a very junior officer trying to get surface warfare qualified, the deck was stacked against me on a carrier, but I tried my hardest to do the right things, be smart and get noticed. Unfortunately, I didn't always succeed.

I actually did well in engineering. The time I spent below deck was fascinating. IKE was a huge operation, but it seemed to make sense to me. Without getting into detail, the reactor basically is an efficient water heater, which creates steam, which drives the turbines and propels the ship.

Fresh water was the lifeblood of IKE and the ship had four water distillers that each produced 100,000 gallons of water a day from seawater. Water is used for human consumption, survival and sanitation, but when we were in flight operations, nearly all of a day's production went to the steam-powered catapults and arresting gear. The distillers were arguably the most important components of the ship. When I spent time in engineering, I noticed that many of the vital pumps in the ship were Union Pumps made in Battle Creek. I was thrilled to see a piece of my hometown as a vital part of the ship.

The USS George Washington was anchored off Haiti after the massive earthquake a few years ago not only for the humanitarian mission of providing helicopter, medical transport and rescue operations, but more important, distilling fresh water that was pumped ashore and that may have saved thousands of lives. No other nation or Navy can do that kind of mission and provide that kind of help.

Knowing engineering was important when you stood bridge watches. You had to know what was going on below deck and how it affected the ship if you were ultimately the Officer of the Deck while the ship was underway.

I got all my engineering qualifications quickly and enjoyed spending time there. I scored high on my test for surface warfare qualifications. Everything down there was logical, orderly and had a purpose. I did struggle to learn the electrical system. Drawing schematics and bus lines was a challenge, but I learned enough to pass.

I stood a lot of bridge watches as the Junior Officer of the Watch, the JOOW. The role of the JOOW was to drive the radar, track and plot passing ships on the maneuvering board and make recommendations to the OOD on whether passing ships posed a threat or if we needed to maneuver to avoid a collision. It was important, but everyone on the bridge sees what's going on; you were the backup. The problem was that many oceangoing merchant ships are on autopilot and may not have an alert bridge team. Add to that, many are on a schedule going from point A to point B and altering course would cost them time and money. Many times we moved when we were the stand-on vessel, despite the rules of the road. Safety was always our first concern. There is also a backup surface watch team in the Combat Information Center (CIC) that relays ship positions to the bridge. They don't have the advantage of seeing from the bridge's perspective, so they often are ignored. That would really bother us when I stood watches as the CIC Surface Watch Officer.

Believe it or not, the route across the Atlantic from Norfolk to Gibraltar is like a highway. With the advent of GPS and precise tracking, many times we were on reciprocal courses with merchant ships coming over the horizon. We would often say that driving the carrier was hours of boredom followed by moments of sheer panic. It was true.

I stood many watches at JOOW and it became old hat. Most of the time, there were few ships to track on the open seas, so you just kept an eye on the radar and out the front window to prevent boredom.

Dolphins to Starboard!

One time, I learned a big lesson on vigilance and attention to detail. We stood watch many times on the bridge during flight operations. It was always exciting to launch and recover aircraft when we were at sea.

Thousands of things had to all go right, every time – everything from the speed of the ship to the wind over the deck to the compression in the catapults and, above all, the care taken with safety procedures. People on the flight deck are constantly told to "keep your head on a swivel." Planes turn and move and a jet blast or prop wash can blow you off the deck in a split second of distraction. A moment's inattention can be fatal. Familiarity often breeds complacency.

And so it was on the bridge. I was standing at my radar station, bored during what seemed like a routine flight operation (they are never routine!) in the Mediterranean. I found myself staring out the window looking forward as planes came and went without incident. With no ships on the horizon and an otherwise normal deck, my mind drifted off.

As I glanced off the starboard bow, like many times before, I noticed dolphins jumping in our bow wake, something that happens frequently. As I started watching them, more and more appeared. Eventually there were dozens and dozens of dolphins. It was unbelievable and rare. I had never seen so many. I picked up the binoculars and started saying, *"Hey look everyone, off the starboard bow. Wow, hundreds of dolphins out there. Have you ever seen so many?! Unbelievable!"*

I kept watching for a few moments and no one seemed interested. I lowered the binoculars and said, *"You guys need to check this out...,"* suddenly realizing something was very wrong. The OOD was giving me the evil eye and I saw the skipper and the air boss conferring. I didn't know what it was about, so I just shut up.

A moment later one of the other watch standers quietly informed me we had an A-7 Corsair, a single-engine jet, with complete hydraulic failure attempting to make an emergency landing. It was touch and go as the pilot fought his aircraft while the boss and skipper debated raising the barricade for emergency landing and recovery.

I had been oblivious to the big picture. As they say, I had "lost the bubble" on situational awareness. I felt like an idiot. The plane landed safely because of everyone's attention to detail – except mine. I later got the proverbial ass-chewing, so common among junior officers. I feared my professional reputation was about to go down the tubes.

My shipmates had a field day with my blunder and gave me the call sign "Flipper." For the next few days, I would walk into the wardroom at meal time and hear the clicking "EEK" sound that Flipper (the only dolphin to have his own TV show) would make. On a few nights, the messenger of the watch would knock on my stateroom door, wake me up and hand me a note from the OOD stating, "Dolphins spotted to starboard, just letting you know!" It was funny for a while, but it drove home the point about attention to detail, something I've never forgotten.

I took the lesson to heart as I finally got my opportunity to drive or "conn" the ship during flight ops. When launching aircraft from a carrier, we needed to have proper wind for flight. To launch and recover, the wind had to be 10 degrees off the port bow at 30 knots to create lift for catapult launch and a headwind at a slow enough speed for the tail hook to catch the arresting wire without stalling when the aircraft landed. In case you missed the wire on landing, you had to have enough speed to lift off and make another attempt. The weight of an F-14 required it go to full throttle as soon as it hit the deck in case the hook didn't catch. As soon as the pilot knew he was hooked, he backed off and came to a stop.

To create the wind, the OOD and conning officer have a Wiz Wheel on the bridge. It's like a slide rule only round and used to check the wind speed and direction; you slide the wheel to a point where you have the needed wind and speed. Once you turn to that course and speed you have to continuously watch the anemometer or wind gauge. You literally end up "chasing the wind" to keep it constant.

It becomes very difficult when a storm is near, because the wind coming from the storm, which is generally circular from the center of the storm, tends to suck you into the storm as you pass it. It wasn't uncommon to get all the planes off just before you drove right into the storm because you would constantly keep steering toward it.

When you make minor adjustments to direction or speed of the ship, you can only do it when a plane is over the deck. Then you are limited to a brief one- to two-degree course change because you don't want to move the airport as another plane is on approach. You don't make adjustments while a plane is on approach, regardless of what the wind is doing.

On that first day of conning flight ops, I was vigilant in keeping the wind direction and speed constant. I stayed very aware of where planes were on their approach and only moved the deck when I should have. I thought I was doing a spectacular job, hoping to earn the praise of the captain, but we had a real prick as the OOD that day. As I was concentrating on the wind and speed, the OOD came over to me and asked me, *"How many more planes to come down?"* I snidely replied, *"I don't know, I'm driving the ship. Ask air ops."* That was the wrong answer and the OOD started berating me in front of the captain.

The captain spun around in his chair after hearing our exchange and said, *"Relieve him!"* I was really pissed because I felt I lost the confidence of the captain at the expense of a brown-nosing OOD.

A few days later I got over it and realized that being on the bridge you had to be aware of everything, even if it "wasn't your job." It was a hard and humiliating lesson to learn in leadership. I realized I needed to study the green sheet better, which has all the details of the flight schedule, and know the entire flight schedule before watch even if I was only the conning officer.

Details are often the difference between life and death in the military.

In hindsight, I was still working as if more planes still had to land, even though the last plane was down. As I thought about it, I looked pretty stupid not knowing I should stand down. I was obsessed with "chasing the wind" and thought I was doing my job, which for the most part I was!

Unfortunately, the competition for watches with a big crew made it difficult for another opportunity on a limited schedule. I never had another chance to prove myself and I always regret that I didn't have the self-confidence to push harder to get the watches.

Lucky to Be Alive

Those of us who have served in the Navy share something many don't understand – sea stories. When we get together, the adventures we shared are rehashed and often embellished over time.

I was standing quarterdeck watch on IKE at Pier 12 as OOD on a beautiful Norfolk day. Several of the aviation squadrons were moving aboard as IKE was getting ready to deploy. The crews come aboard, set up shop and get underway with the ship. As the ship gets out to sea, the air wing flies the aircraft aboard. Depending on the aircraft, they came from Naval Air Stations Norfolk, Oceana and Jacksonville. A few of the EA-6Bs, the electronic warfare modified versions of the A-6 Intruder, flew from Washington state.

During that quarterdeck watch, my fraternity brother from CMU, Rick Vanden Heuvel, came walking up the bow to report aboard. "Hoover," as he was named by his gunny sergeant at AOCS in Pensacola because Vanden Heuvel was too complicated, was reporting aboard to join the E-2C Squadron, the Bluetails of VAW-121, which was part of IKE's carrier air wing. We were excited to see each other and it looked like we would be sailing together on his first deployment. We spent a lot of liberty together and I got to know many of his squadron mates.

Hoover had joined the Navy a year earlier after struggling with an unfulfilling sales position with Campbell Soup in Kalamazoo, just west of Battle Creek. We got together a few times while he was in Kalamazoo. In his spare time, he picked up his private pilot's license and I flew with him on occasion doing aerial photography. His father was a retired Navy captain and he decided to become a naval aviator and set off for Aviation Officer Candidate School in Pensacola.

By the time I entered the Navy in Newport, he had finished up at AOCS and was headed to flight training, which ended up at the E-2C Training Command at Naval Air Station Norfolk, VAW-120. He was on his way to becoming an E-2C Naval Flight Officer or NFO. The E-2 is the command and control aircraft with the large radar dome that coordinates the operations from the sky. Today, it is still the only propeller-driven aircraft flown from a carrier. It is always the first plane off the deck in flight ops and the last to return.

The training command in Norfolk was known as the Readiness Air Group, or "RAG." It's where a trainee had a first chance to learn about and fly a specialty

Ensign T.R. Shaw and his CMU fraternity brother Lieutenant JG Rick (Hoover) Vanden Heuvel during their first cruise in the Navy. Vanden Heuvel was in Airborne Early Warning Squadron (VAW-121) flying the E-2C Hawkeye. They deployed together for the USS Eisenhower's Mediterranean cruise in 1983. (U.S. Navy photo)

craft. As an E-2C NFO or "Mole," Hoover would be one of three junior officers working the radars in the back of the plane. I was lucky enough to attend his winging ceremony at the Breezy Point Officers Club when he finished flight training. A tradition when getting your wings was chugging a pitcher of beer with your wings at the bottom and catching them with your teeth before you could put them on. It was a testament to the days when nearly every social event in the Navy centered around hard drinking. Unlike surface officers, aviators get their wings before their first operational squadron tour and must continue their qualifications to keep them. They didn't have the stress of earning them, but lived with the threat of losing them. Getting your Surface Warfare pin came at the end after proving yourself and getting the pin was the goal. Once you had it, you were qualified. Two starkly different approaches to qualification.

One night on IKE, Hoover was flying in the back of the E-2C while I was standing bridge watch. Like I've said, nothing is routine with flight ops and at night it's even more treacherous on the flight deck.

I was standing watch, primarily monitoring the surface radar and making recommendations for course changes if we were going to get too close to another ship. In the open ocean, it's usually slow and we have the advantage of seeing other ships with our "height of eye" on the carrier.

At night, the bridge is dark to preserve our night vision. As planes make their approach to the ship, a camera facing aft in the deck near the arresting wires allows bridge officers to see planes approach on the monitor. The plane constantly grows larger until it flies over the camera and lands. The camera has crosshairs so you can see if the plane is high, low or off center. The recording of the approach is often used in debrief and training to improve accuracy on approach. At night, the camera is very light sensitive as it picks up the light of the incoming plane at a great distance. The glow of the TV monitor grows brighter as the plane approaches.

That night an E-2, which Hoover was in, was making its approach as the last plane on deck. The monitor is on the far left of the bridge over the captain's chair. I glanced up and could see the plane approaching and looked forward and down at the flight deck. At that moment there were nearly 100 sailors on the deck cleaning up and moving planes just in front of the bridge tower.

All of a sudden, there was a flash of light on the bridge. I looked up at the monitor and saw the starboard engine of the E-2 flame out on approach and it lit up the bridge with the light sensitive camera in the deck. I saw the E-2 yaw right out of the screen. For a moment I wondered, *"Where did it go?"*

Then, a second later I saw the belly of the plane pass by the port window of the bridge. We could see the rivets on the bottom of the plane.

A pilot rolled the plane 90 degrees so it wouldn't clip the tower with the starboard wing and then rolled level again and went off over the starboard bow of the ship just missing the king post. I saw the plane roll back to level and go off descending into the darkness as the lights on the plane flickered and died. I honestly thought it was going in the water just ahead and to the right of the ship. We couldn't see it in the darkness.

The OOD ordered the ship to come left as he and everyone else thought it was in the water.

The captain, who was on the bridge, shouted, *"Hold your course!"* as he was listening to the cockpit chatter. He was cool for such a harrowing situation. Fortunately, the seasoned skipper of the squadron, Cmdr. Johnny Roberts, was sitting in the right seat as co-pilot when this happened. He took control, rolled the plane and pulled it up on one engine in the darkness. His experience and calm saved the lives of hundreds on the ship, including all of us on the bridge. Had he not rolled the plane 90 degrees, the starboard wing would have clipped the tower, caused a horrific crash, and wiped out most of the airmen on the deck below, and forward of the bridge, as well as those of us on the bridge. It was a remarkable feat. The E-2 came around again and landed on one engine. The squadron skipper earned a well-deserved Air Medal.

The NFOs in the back of the E-2 had blown the escape hatch and were ready to ditch if it hit the water. Everyone breathed a huge sigh of relief!

I was told when the skipper regained control, he asked if everyone is all right in back, they responded, "*We're OK skipper, just need some new pants!*"

D-Day 1984

One of the most memorable events on IKE was the 40th anniversary of D-Day in Normandy, France. The USS Eisenhower, being a namesake ship along with the USS Montgomery, made a port call to Portsmouth, England, in early June 1984 and on June 6, 1984, crossed the English Channel and landed in Brest, France, where the ship and crew joined in many ceremonies honoring the liberating invasion 40 years earlier in 1944.

The ship's senior leaders took part in formal events at sites of historical significance. The rest of us waited for liberty and visited many of the places we had read and heard about.

A few weeks before the port visit, the star-studded D-Day movie "The Longest Day" was played several times over the ship's broadcast system. It gave younger sailors a chance to learn far more about D-Day than we might have in high school or college classes.

We finally had liberty call in northern France and took advantage of tours. Several of us visited Omaha Beach and other landing beaches where the Allied troops had come ashore in German-occupied Normandy. I had a strange feeling that if I dug into the sand, I might find blood. We also visited Sainte-Mere-Eglise, the town where paratroopers first landed and actor Mickey Rooney had played the young soldier who got hung up in the church steeple and watched the battle from his chute for several hours.

We visited Point Du Hoc where Army Rangers scaled the near impossible cliff to overrun the German battery. To stand at the top and look down, one would swear there was no way possible they could have done it.

That was a day when everything was possible.

The tour ended with a visit to the U.S. Cemetery at Normandy, one of the few National Cemeteries outside of the United States. It looks like most National Cemeteries with white markers, crosses and Stars of David in perfect alignment.

As I started walking down the rows, I couldn't help but notice nearly all the dates of death were the same: June 6, 1944. That's when the emotions hit me and I began to cry. I was overcome by the realization of what all I had seen that day and the sacrifices so many young Americans made for the world's freedom. It changed me forever.

Following the deployment, which remained uneventful, we returned to

Norfolk. I tried hard to get my Surface Warfare pin, but it eluded me on this cruise. I wasn't sure what I would do as IKE was going to the yard and wouldn't be underway again for a long time.

Lesson Learned

For nearly two years on IKE, I tried as hard as I could to get my Surface Warfare Qualification. I saw good officers come and go and made great friends. I loved carrier life, but didn't like being a junior surface officer in an aviation world. I was slowly progressing, but I wasn't the best junior officer on the ship and I struggled to compete for duty and watches. I suffered from junior officer syndrome, where I felt I could do little right and confidence eluded me.

It was also difficult being away from home for long periods of time. In those days we didn't have the Internet or cell phones. Communication with home was rare. I spent a lot of my spare time reading and learning as much as I could, but many days I could only take so much Navy thought. I spent entire days **Defying the Immediate** and fighting boredom as the monotony of daily life at sea took its toll.

As the ship went into the yard for extended periods, I was counseled to find a cross deck opportunity and I did. I got orders to the USS Charleston (LKA 113), an amphibious ship in Norfolk, and I was excited to keep charging. I remember another officer suggesting that I ask my new skipper how I could become his best officer! I was ready for a fresh start. I didn't want to blow it, but I soon found that problems followed me.

CHAPTER 11

No. 1 Chuck

"Sometimes the transition from being in control of your life to having absolutely no control is swift, but other times it is so gradual that you wonder exactly when it truly began."
— Mickey Rooney

IKE was heading to the shipyard at the end of our last deployment for a Complex Overhaul (COH), which meant it would be months before it would be underway again. That meant no more time to reach my qualifications. I had heard stories about working on a ship while it's undergoing COH. For many it's a welcome time at home and getting to know your family again despite the dirty and noisy environment of a shipyard. For some, it was time to pursue education. In hindsight, I wish I had done that.

I was eager to get surface warfare qualified so I asked about "cross-decking" where you would be assigned to another ship because IKE didn't need a full crew in the shipyard. My request led to my first experience with a detailer, the Navy's personnel department. My exit interview from IKE was with Capt. Dick Macke, and I brought up how hard it was for a junior surface officer on IKE. He pondered how we could make it better for others who would follow me. Maybe he was isolated from what really went on, but I always wondered if anything changed after I left. It may have, but I left not feeling like I really made a difference. But after all I had been through, I was ready for a new challenge.

The detailers assigned me to the USS Charleston (LKA 113), the lead ship of the Charleston class amphibious cargo ship, which was at the end of its time in the Portsmouth Navy Shipyard. It was moored at its special place on the Norfolk waterfront at the end of the piers. Capt. J.T. Murphy, the CO, got that spot as a favor; it had a lot of parking, was quiet and wasn't near a lot of the activity of the destroyer and submarine piers to the north.

After some time off, I reported to the Charleston, excited for a new opportunity to prove myself. Now with two years of fleet experience, much was expected of me. I was assigned as 3rd Division Officer or the Boat Group

Commander in the Deck Department. The title at least sounded impressive! The division owned the four LCM-8 boats, the amphibious landing boat with a bow ramp for driving vehicles on shore. It was big enough to hold an M-1 tank.

The Charleston is basically a transport ship with giant booms and 70-ton cranes for transporting supplies and vehicles to support an amphibious landing, which will likely never happen in this modern age of warfare. The "Mike boats" sit atop the cargo holds on the main deck in transit and our division maintained them.

I had never been around the amphibious Navy, so I had much to learn. Shortly after I got there, my chief, an engineman, and a couple of boatswain's mates went to the Little Creek Amphibious Base where one of our boats was being repaired. I went along to ride the Mike boat back down the bay to the ship. It was my first experience with small craft, with the exception of riding the liberty boats on IKE and getting tossed around in high seas during a man-overboard drill in a motor whale boat. I was there to learn and observe and let the chief and crew show me how it worked.

After getting a rundown, we boarded and headed out of the cove at Little Creek and onto the Chesapeake Bay.

About halfway there, the boat stopped – dead in the water. After several attempts to start it, the engineman started looking around the engine compartment. At this point I was clueless on how it worked, so I just let them tinker. Then I asked, *"Have you checked the fuel?"* The engineman opened the gas tank, dropped a sounding weight down and it came up bone dry. We were out of gas. He hadn't checked it before getting underway.

We were adrift in Chesapeake Bay. At the time we didn't have radios on the small craft, so we had to hail a fisherman who radioed our distress to the harbormaster at Little Creek. About 30 minutes later, the tug came out and towed us back. By the time we fueled up and got started again, we were way behind schedule.

The first lieutenant, head of the Deck Department, was rightfully pissed off and we heard about it. I got my first ass-chewing on the Charleston and it didn't put me in a favorable light with Capt. Murphy. I was senior on the boat and apparently should have known better, but I trusted the crew who I assumed were well-trained and responsible. It was another hard lesson about accountability and command.

Unfortunately, a pattern was developing as I quickly learned that many of the sailors I would be working with weren't the best or brightest. Bad things were happening, many of which weren't my fault. As much as I struggled on the carrier, the level of competence of everyone on IKE was far greater. Perhaps it's because life or death situations were frequent and aviators have a heightened sense of what's critical and important. I was constantly shaking my head and wondering what I was getting into. The Surface Navy wasn't what I was expecting, but I pressed on doing the best I could.

Charleston was often underway. We took the ship up and down the East Coast and went for refresher training (REFTRA) at the Navy's Guantanamo Bay base in Cuba. Guantanamo is a great deep water port and we have a huge training command there. It's a warm weather destination where we took the ship in and out of port and really did lot of intense training. There was not much liberty because everything was on the base.

One evening several officers went to dinner with Capt. Murphy at the Guantanamo Officers Club. We took the captain's gig across the bay and had drinks and dinner. We learned a little about each other and the skipper, a gentlemanly officer who had enjoyed a long career that was nearing an end. Charleston was his final tour. I wished he could have stayed longer – things would have been much different – but the Navy is a revolving door of leadership. I got along well with him. His relief was a seismic shift in personality and leadership.

Working in the Deck Department and running the boats was a challenge. My boss, the first lieutenant, was an LDO who didn't care much for college boys. He was a former boatswain's mate who liked to make things difficult for traditional junior officers. He often said, *"I got my commission the hard way. I earned it!"* I tried hard but apparently got off on the wrong foot. I also made the mistake of relying too much on my chiefs and petty officers because they had the experience and knew what to do. Somewhere in training I remember learning about trusting your chief, which I did far too often!

One day the first lieutenant took me and my chief aside and looked over our boats. He started rattling off all the things that needed to be done. I listened but didn't write anything down. Big mistake. He got nitpicky about what color the handles were supposed to have been painted. I had my shields up because I thought he was being facetious and cocky, so I kept my mouth shut, agreed and said OK. I once again assumed the chief knew what needed to be done and would make it happen. The problem was that every time something wasn't right, I was the one who got the ass-chewing. It all goes back to accountability, something I was having a tough time with because I wasn't the one doing the physical work. I wasn't seeing that I really had to step up and be a leader in my division.

I found it hard to be assertive and that needed to change. When I tried to be a hard-ass it came off as fake and uninspiring. I was beginning to think I wasn't cut out for this; I could never be the prick I needed to be to get things done. I felt like my superiors thought I was weak and ineffective.

When we came back from Guantanamo, we spent several weeks at home. The ship went into Portsmouth for minor repairs. We had a long stretch before deploying and I went to several schools at Little Creek. I took a course in how all our booms and cargo handling devices worked, learned about amphibious warfare and some small boat seamanship. It was fun.

I also took a course to become a Landing Signal Officer or LSO. Since I had carrier experience, I was also given the collateral job of Flight Deck Officer when we had flight quarters. Charleston had a helicopter deck on the stern and I ran the control tower during helo transfers, which we did frequently. The flight ops came easily to me and I could actually be in control of something on the ship with competent people. I was responsible for communications with the bridge and helicopters, kept an eye on the wind and ensured safe flight operation. I was proud that on our Mediterranean deployment we completed more than 1,000 safe helicopter evolutions. I had no one bugging me and felt I was actually in control of something on the ship. It was my favorite part of serving on Charleston. When I ran into friends from IKE I could tell them I was the "air boss."

Just after we came out of the shipyard, Capt. Murphy retired. We were only back at the pier a few days and had to shift from a frantic shipyard environment to normal pier-side operations and ready the ship for a change of command. The ship was filthy!

The ceremony was to take place in the middle cargo hold, one of my spaces. We worked hard to clean and prep it for the big event under tough circumstances and in a short time frame. We thought we did a great job.

The day of the event, the ceremony went off well. None of us had a chance to meet the new skipper before the ceremony, so we mingled in the wardroom afterward and went through all the perfunctory greetings. None of us knew much about the skipper, except that as a former submariner he had a dolphin pin. The Navy has many communities – Surface, Air, Sub, Supply, Intel, etc. This was my first experience with a "bubblehead" as we called them, and the common understanding was that submariners could be uptight and demanding. We were about to find out.

During this reception, before I even personally met my new boss, the first lieutenant told me to get in my working khakis, and have the chief muster the troops. I questioned it as it was late in the afternoon and most everyone was getting ready for a well-deserved liberty call after working two days to clean the ship. *"What's going on?"* I asked. *"You'll find out soon enough,"* he replied.

Puzzled, we gathered on the main deck near where the ladder leads down to the cargo hold. The new skipper came down and began tearing into us about how embarrassed he was by the condition of our spaces. We gave each other puzzled looks, thinking we had done a stellar job.

He pointed out how dirty the main deck was and then pointed to a boat fender that was partially deflated and looked horrible. He took us down the ladder and pointed out dirt in the corners and crevasses that we had missed. He found masking tape that hadn't been removed after painting.

Yes, there were a few things we missed, but our goal was to make the cargo hold immaculate, which it was. What we missed were some entry points. It seemed minor considering what we started with.

Without much of a welcome aboard, he cancelled liberty for my division and demanded we get the ship cleaned up. Angrily, he reiterated how embarrassed he was by the ship's condition. We thought he was way out of line and had chosen a terrible way to begin his tour as our leader. What an unappreciative bastard, we all thought. If he had seen what it looked like 48 hours earlier, he would have understood.

My job in the next moment was to quell anger and get the cleanup completed as quickly as possible. The skipper had made a terrible first impression on all of us and shown the worst kind of leadership. From that point on, our guards were up. Things weren't going to get easier.

The first lieutenant and I knew it would be a challenge with this guy and things only got worse. When I was on IKE, the aviators joked that the Surface Navy "eats their young." After this incident it was clear what they meant.

I feared I'd never be on his good side and likely was doomed as a junior officer. My fears were pretty much realized later on.

We got underway and did workups for an upcoming deployment to the Mediterranean. One of the exercises we did was in North Carolina where we had a mock landing on the beach. Several ships in our group, which all had small boats, organized an amphibious landing on Onslow Beach near Parris Island. I was the boat officer on an LCM-8 doing a night landing.

We all formed up, in total darkness, and drove toward the beach where we would beach the boat and lower the ramp. Our mission was to pick up evacuees, several volunteers who we would basically load up and bring to the ship. As we drove toward shore there were a few amphibious craft ahead of us, so I knew the beach was still ahead. Without radar, I had no perspective on where we were. As long as the LARCs, amphibious personnel carriers, were in front of us, we hadn't reached the beach, I reasoned.

In total darkness, we suddenly heard "thunk," hitting the beach at too slow a speed. A wave picked us up and we broached sideways onto the beach, making a humiliating and ugly landing, something no officer wants to do.

It turns out that the LARCs in front of us were already 100 yards onto the beach. As soon as they hit, they could drive up with their six big wheels. What they failed to do was turn off their underway running lights. That's why I assumed they hadn't landed. When they turned on their headlights after we broached, it was clear that they were on the beach. I was pissed; we didn't get up enough speed to land because I thought we weren't at the beach. I anticipated another ass-chewing, which I later received. I was beginning to really hate this surface Navy stuff.

I felt I became a problematic officer around the ship. I had the feeling that all the commanders were thinking, *"What will Shaw screw up next?"* Eventually, I got sick of not being able to overcome my reputation. I didn't have a passion for running the boats or working with deck sailors any longer, so I took an opportunity to become the ship's administrative officer.

Administration was more my speed and aptitude. It was a great job and I had the executive officer as a buffer between me and the skipper. I published the Plan of the Day and became the collateral duty public affairs officer. I got along well with the XO. I had a small division of a couple yeomen and a senior chief personnelman. The ship's postal clerk was also in my division, and he was the hardest working person on the ship. Mail was vitally important and he nearly spent 24/7 doing postal work; he was pretty autonomous. We all worked together well and I excelled as an executive, running a small team. I was in my element, but it was never enough to elevate me in the eyes of the superiors. I got some ink in the local military press and did a good job as PAO. I should have pursued the field then, but was working under the assumption I still needed my surface warfare pin first.

In Deck Department, no matter how hard I tired, nothing worked out well for me. I now had a manageable team with a mission I could excel at and I thought I did. Things were looking better, but surface warfare qualification was still eluding me.

I continued standing watches in both the CIC and on the bridge and got to do more ship handling although I never became a full-fledged OOD underway. I wasn't trusted, and I never really pushed hard to do it.

I never made a connection with the skipper and he became someone to avoid. Being junior, I was intimidated. Several of the department heads warmed up to him, but only for professional survival. Several of them had dealt with leaders like him before and were professionally cautious, knowing he wouldn't last forever. In private, many couldn't stand him and kept a poker face around him.

It didn't take long to begin to think that this skipper had a drinking problem. When we were in port, he would take long lunch breaks at the officers' club, return to the ship, and disappear to his stateroom, only to come out at liberty call, chew people out, cancel their liberty and go home.

Throughout this time with his inconsistent and abrasive leadership, the crew's morale deteriorated. It became hard to get anyone to do much of anything on the ship. I remember hearing deck seamen joking about the captain and I had to chastise them when I heard it. That was not an appropriate way to talk about a senior, but I understood their frustration.

For a long time, he neglected qualifying people for watches and duty. As admin officer, I sent up several qualification packages and letters that piled up on his sofa.

Once he tried to take a chief petty officer to captain's mast for "gun-decking" (falsifying) maintenance records, which was absurd. That completely burned his bridge to the chief's mess, the vital middle managers in the Navy. He backed off, but was no longer respected by the chiefs – a position no commanding officer wants to be in.

Many of the junior officers, myself included, felt powerless to do anything. The department heads weren't willing to jeopardize their careers and would rather put up with the situation than rock the boat. The junior officers didn't know who was on the captain's side, or if they were enabling him, so we couldn't complain or express our frustration to them. Nobody wanted to be a whistleblower. Besides, who'd believe us?

I always felt I had a target on my back and was blamed for things I didn't deserve. I felt I no longer had a future in the Surface Navy or on active duty and looked forward to completing my obligated service and reevaluating my career. And my life!

Fortunately, I decided to continue in the Navy Reserve after leaving active duty – a decision I never regretted. As part of the transition program, I attended a seminar that told us all about the reserve and why it made sense to continue our careers.

With Norfolk behind me, I felt I was finally safe from any repercussion, so I wrote to the admiral who was the Amphibious Group Commander about the skipper and the condition and morale of the ship. It was worrisome since I didn't want to come off as a washed-out junior officer with sour grapes. The admiral responded, simply thanking me for bringing it to his attention. It seemed perfunctory. I didn't know then if I actually had done the right thing, or if it did any good.

I never found out exactly what happened to the skipper. I was told a new, well-liked skipper came aboard and righted the ship, restoring the crew's morale. If I had stuck it out, I may have salvaged my active duty career.

But that phase of my life was over. It was time to move on.

Unfortunately, the USS Charleston was on her last leg and would soon be decommissioned, as amphibious warfare was becoming archaic. The new skipper would be the last to command the ship. The "Number One Chuck" now sits rusting in the Philadelphia Shipyard beside her sister ship the USS El Paso, (LKA 117), whose former skipper was Capt. Roy Cash, a former Top Gun commander and nephew of legendary singer Johnny Cash. While Cash commanded El Paso, his daughter Kellye Cash became Miss America 1987.

A new USS Charleston, (LCS 18), an Independence Class littoral combat ship, was built, christened in 2017 and commissioned in February 2019 in her namesake city in South Carolina. She is the sixth ship to bear the name.

Lesson Learned

I began my tour on the USS Charleston full of hope, determination and vigor.

As things outside my control began happening, my reputation faded and I found it hard to gain favor with anyone senior to me. A few times I was a victim of political gamesmanship, but other times I just didn't have the right knowledge. I often learned things too late to make a difference. I grew frustrated and felt I couldn't progress, no matter how hard I tried. I made the fatal decision that the deck was stacked against me and pretty much stopped trying.

I felt that I was striving for an unattainable goal. I knew there was an end in sight and it made no sense to keep beating my head against the wall. My goal became surviving until my term of service was complete. It was a terrible way to end an active Navy career.

Hindsight is 20/20.

Throughout my officer training, the idea of accountability was constantly repeated. As officers, we have a moral obligation to look out for the best interest of our crew, our ship and the Navy, regardless of rank. As junior officers we felt powerless to do anything about a bad situation involving a senior.

I came to understand how hard it is to be a whistleblower in any organization. I also came to realize juniors had more power than we realized. Many officers on the ship had the power to do something about the situation, but couldn't muster the courage to do so. Nearly all of us took the path of least resistance and let a bad situation fester. Many of us had the power, and the AUTHORITY, to do something, but not the courage.

My active duty career ended without surface warfare qualification and I went on to find redemption in the Navy Reserve.

I Defied the Immediate and went on in spite of an awful professional situation. Life often offers second chances, but my hope was to find new life as a citizen-sailor reservist. And I did!

CHAPTER 12

Homeport Battle Creek

"When I go home, it's an easy way to be grounded. You learn to realize what truly matters."
— Tony Stewart, race car driver

While in transition from active duty, we listened to a lecture on the Navy Reserve and it resonated with me – the importance of keeping your career alive and serving as a part-time sailor. I knew there was a Navy Reserve center in Battle Creek and it worked perfectly for me. I could serve close to home, maintain my Navy ties and pursue an undetermined civilian career.

With Norfolk in my rearview mirror, I was excited to start fresh on a Navy career. I was a senior lieutenant (junior grade). I figured there couldn't be many officers drilling in Battle Creek, so I might have some seniority. I was dead wrong! An overwhelming majority of Navy recruits and officers come from mid-America, the nation's heartland. When they leave active duty, as I did, they come home to serve as reservists close to home.

On reporting to Battle Creek, I stood on the drill deck for my first morning muster and gazed across a sea of gold stripes. Commanders and captains, three and four stripers and lots of them! I soon discovered that Battle Creek was home to several staff and medical units comprised of many officers. I also learned that the entire reserve force was top-heavy as many sought to finish an active career. *"Oh crap, I'm still junior!"* I thought.

Serving in the reserve was a welcome respite from my civilian job-hunting. I was still trying to figure out my next career move and working part-time at the funeral home. When I started, I was not fully committed to funeral service, so reserve duty paid a little and gave me connections with other professionals. I soon discovered that the reserve force was full of top-notch people with business connections throughout the Midwest. Reservists came to Battle Creek from Michigan, Indiana, Wisconsin, Ohio and Illinois.

I was immediately assigned as executive officer to an amphibious construction battalion (SEABEES) whose home unit was back at Little Creek Amphibious Base in Virginia Beach. We visited the base once a quarter with all the other nationwide reserve units and joined in exercises that included building an ELCAS or "Elevated Causeway" – a 1,500-foot pier for an amphibious beachhead and landing when no port facilities existed. We operated small boats and construction equipment. The unit was made up mostly of blue-collar sailors who were proud SEABEES.

Our mission, besides building piers, was to offload ships of the Maritime Prepositioning Force. MPF is a group of fully-loaded merchant ships that sailed the world at the ready to deliver supplies and equipment. They frequently deployed to hot spots awaiting a mission. When they came to Little Creek, we unloaded and resupplied them. When Operation Desert Shield and Desert Storm began, the U.S. contracted with the United Arab Emirates for a pier head and port facility, rendering our mission obsolete.

Still, I felt good with the title of XO, but I had a lot to learn. Outside their reserve obligations, most of the enlisted sailors worked in construction fields or as steelworkers, heavy equipment operators, truck drivers and in other labor fields with a few experienced boatswain's mates and enginemen thrown in. My skipper, Commander John Guidinger, was an old salt who served in Vietnam and was nearing retirement. Fortunately, he took me under his wing and I learned all about working in the reserve force.

Not long after affiliating with the Navy Reserve, I was promoted to full lieutenant, which felt good. I eventually rose to lieutenant commander, but full commander eluded me as I eventually moved to public affairs and had to compete with others who had served longer in that field.

One of my exercises was an overnight on the beach at Little Creek. We set up a camp as if we had made a landing on a foreign shore. We built a perimeter defense and operated a headquarters on the beach directing gear coming ashore. For a day or so, we ate MREs (Meals Ready to Eat or Meals Rejected by Ethiopia!) It was a lot of fun, but after several years aboard ships, it seemed like I was in the Army or Marine Corps.

We spent most drill weekends in Battle Creek on administrative details and training. By comparison, our weekends in Tidewater were for four days of real training at the command and I found them fun and often adventurous. On one excursion, I was, as second in command, the skipper with about 30 sailors. The CO couldn't attend and left me in charge. It was a challenge making sure they all got to where they needed to be. Most had flown on the airlines, but a few hadn't, so we all needed to look out for one another. Many of the young sailors came directly into the reserve for their skills and never served on active duty or traveled on military orders.

One night when we all arrived at Little Creek, there was no berthing (beds) available. I scrambled to find lodging for the night and do the paperwork for reimbursement. About a third of the sailors didn't have credit cards, further complicating the situation. It became an administrative nightmare, but we eventually worked things out.

The next drill weekend, I took credit card applications with me and did a presentation on credit and financial responsibility. We insisted that everyone have a valid credit card to travel with the Navy. Eventually, the Navy got smart and issued a government credit card for travel through an agreement with Bank of America. I used it several times during my career and was always guarded with its use. It made things easier, but for some sailors it was like putting candy in their hands.

One of my sailors was a living version of the Peanuts character Pig Pen. He would arrive for training unprepared – his uniforms were never right. He didn't bring a jacket, so he wore the camouflage utility jacket, which we weren't supposed to travel in. At the airport on the way home, he set off the metal detector because he had several shell casings from the range in his coat pocket. He was pulled aside and thoroughly searched, almost making us miss our flight home. Oh, the joys of command!

One of our active duty company commanders at Little Creek, Lt. Mike Thornton, was a legendary figure in the Navy. At that time, he was the only Medal of Honor recipient on active duty. He earned the honor for heroic action as a Navy Seal during the Vietnam War. A statue of him carrying his teammate, Lt. Tommy Norris, who he rescued, stands outside the UDT/SEAL Museum in Fort Pierce, Florida. Norris also had received a Medal of Honor for his actions earlier in Vietnam.

Thornton was the Bravo Company commander in charge of all the small boats at the command when I served there. He was one of the humblest officers I ever worked with.

A lesson I quickly learned in the reserve – never spend too much time in one unit. As you progress in rank, Navy brass look for diversity and leadership when they consider promotions. The rule of thumb is to never spend more than two or three years in the same unit. Every year you can apply for a new billet and possible command of a unit. I spent four years with the SEABEES, so some senior officers encouraged me to take another unit. With the SEABEES, I served as both executive and commanding officer.

At the time, the Navy Reserve created a sub-command at the Reserve Center called a Surface Readiness Unit (SRU). It was headed by Capt. Wayne Kruger and he oversaw several other units. He offered me command of a Destroyer Squadron staff unit that had a chief and five enlisted sailors. I eagerly accepted! I was a skipper again and thought it would look good. I had command, at least, at the Reserve Center. The unit was created to augment a Destroyer Squadron staff at Norfolk, but I don't think they knew we existed. I tried to get my sailors to Norfolk, but we faced bureaucracy in getting orders and assignments. It was frustrating, but my command of the unit earned praise.

Another unit under the SRU was the reserve detachment for the USS Peterson (DD 969), which had a relationship with the ship, a Spruance class destroyer. Many of the reservists were trained on the Peterson. I worked out a deal with the unit's skipper to get on the Peterson and, hopefully, finally get my Surface Warfare Board in my two-week tour. I just needed to prove myself on the bridge and sit for a board. The ship's skipper was happy and eager to help but after wrestling with the admin office, my orders never were cut.

An interesting side note: A few years ago, I was watching a "60 Minutes" segment on the Nautilus Project, an underwater environmental exploration using robotics in the Gulf of Mexico. While exploring the Gulf floor, they stumbled across a fairly new sunken Navy ship. The Navy often scuttles ships to dispose of them and create artificial reefs. The ship they discovered at more than 7,000 feet was the USS Peterson! After decommissioning, it was sunk in 2004. I was surprised and excited to see it underwater. It was mind-boggling to think that ship had a connection to Battle Creek and I had a near opportunity to serve on it.

A few years earlier, I tried to get my qualifications on a minesweeper in Seattle. I had answered an offer to come to the ship, get underway and possibly get my SWO pin. I corresponded with the skipper of the USS Pledge (MSO 492) and looked forward to the opportunity. I got orders and traveled to Seattle only to find the ship in dry dock at Lake Union. Three other reservists were there and the CO apologized for being unable to get underway. We spent two weeks in a hotel and being on the ship was a 9-5 job. Still, we found projects to tackle and some of us brought some expertise and conducted training for the crew. All of us were motivated and took advantage of an unfortunate situation and made the best of it.

Later, I had another opportunity to pursue my pin. I did two weeks on the USS Guadalcanal (LPH 7), an amphibious aircraft carrier. I arrived in Norfolk and rode the ship to Guantanamo Bay for their refresher training. I got to conn the ship and complete many underway evolutions, but the operational tempo didn't permit a board for the three junior officers aboard and the qualification eluded me once again.

The first few years of my career in the reserves, I tried hard to get my surface warfare pin, seeking opportunities and experiences beyond my assigned duties, but the odds were against me. At that point, I concentrated on being a good reservist.

The reservists and especially the officers included many individuals who enjoyed success in their civilian jobs but refused to abandon their Navy careers. Among us, we described the reserve force as *"a group of highly skilled, underpaid and motivated patriots who are called upon in a crisis to save the active duty ass!"* There was much truth to the saying that I would come to more fully appreciate in my next unit. After a few years going nowhere with the destroyer squadron, I wasn't selected for command of another unit I applied for and I was asked to join the premier unit at the Battle Creek Reserve Center. The senior leaders there liked me and I was a local guy. They knew my background struggling to get qualified, but joining a staff unit, it didn't matter that much. I had more than enough Navy experience to make substantial contributions to the unit.

I was asked to join SACLANT, an acronym for Supreme Allied Commander Atlantic, the NATO command at the center. This unit had many experienced, well-educated captains and commanders, the best and brightest at the center. I was a senior lieutenant, but one of the most junior officers in the unit. My title was assistant training officer. Not long after joining the unit, I was promoted to lieutenant commander.

Drill weekends were full of heady discussion and research on NATO issues. I was eager to learn about the North Atlantic Treaty Organization. I devoured the NATO handbook and studied relentlessly. The unit frequently did two weeks in Brussels, Belgium, NATO Headquarters or Norfolk, Virginia, the SACLANT Headquarters. I made several trips to SACLANT in Norfolk, but didn't make it across the pond until my next tour with the unit.

One of the fun things I did was organize country briefs. I assigned each member of the unit to brief us on the background, role and developments in one of the NATO nations. I did three nations myself. It was a blast!

During one of my trips to Norfolk as a reservist, I invited my girlfriend Kathy to spend a few days in my old stomping grounds. We had a great time sightseeing, but it was the right time and place to take the plunge.

I had purchased an engagement ring and decided to propose near the ocean at the First Landing site on Cape Henry, which is now part of Fort Story. The site has a cross dedicated to the original landing site of the Jamestown expedition in April 1607 at the southern mouth of Chesapeake Bay. It was a place of historical significance – the site where the settlers' first prayer was conducted and a small cross was erected as the Virginia Company, led by John Smith, consecrated the New World. One historian described it as "Act One, Scene One" in the story of colonizing America.

I was a naval officer proposing to my future wife. We sat and stared at the ocean and bay for the longest time nervously chit-chatting. I kept waiting for us to be alone and the longer I waited, the harder it became. As we were getting ready to leave, we walked to the car. "Hey, let's check out that cross," I suggested. Then, I mustered the nerve, took a knee at the large granite cross and proposed. She accepted and I was about to get a Navy wife! We think we both made the right choice – our marriage is still going strong!

Kathy and I met when I served on the CMU Alumni Association Board in 1996 and organized a golf outing in Battle Creek. She volunteered to help. Kathy had graduated from CMU a few years ahead of me and had moved back to the area several months earlier. She had a sales position and wanted to get involved in community events. She later told me she almost hung up on that phone call because I was puzzled as to why she wanted to help out when she didn't play golf!

Kathy's undergraduate degree was in broadcasting and cinematic arts and she later earned a master's degree at California State University-Fresno. She had worked in production for television stations in Syracuse, Phoenix and Fresno before returning to Michigan and a new career.

Raised on a farm near Marshall – just east of Battle Creek – she bought the family farmhouse from her parents, Arthur and Helen Banfield, when they retired and moved into town. Being a farm girl, she had a strong work ethic and an independent spirit, which made us click.

While at CMU in the mid-1970s she worked for the campus television station and also was a volunteer statistician at Chippewa football games. Back then, she needed special permission from the athletic director to be in the male-only press box. That was among the things igniting her passion for women's rights and equality.

She eventually became involved with the American Association of University Women and became president of the Marshall branch. She later became president of the Michigan AAUW.

After we married in 2000, she worked in the funeral home office and became involved in community affairs. She served on the board and chaired the Music Center of South Central Michigan, which oversees several organizations, including the Battle Creek Symphony Orchestra. She also serves on committees of the Battle Creek Community Foundation and the Winship Foundation, awarding scholarships to local youth.

Back to the reserves.

I was enjoying my time in SACLANT, drilling at home and getting chances to travel. I was with the unit five years, which meant that I had become a homesteader – the dreaded affliction of reserves who remain in the same posting too long. I witnessed at least four skippers take charge of the unit, including then Commander Dirk Debbink, an extremely squared-away Naval Academy graduate and inspiring officer. Debbink ultimately rose to three-star vice admiral, was activated, and served three years as commander of the Navy Reserve Force before retiring in Wisconsin where he owns a large construction company. Debbink later became the chairman of the USS Milwaukee (LCS-5) commissioning committee.

A few years ago, while driving in Wisconsin, I stopped at the famous Mars Cheese Castle, a well-known cultural landmark, during its massive reconstruction along I-94. I was excited to see that Debbink's company was the general contractor.

The Battle Creek SACLANT detachment also had the command's only public affairs officer billet. We had several designated PAOs come through the unit and I learned a lot from them. With my journalism background, I did a lot of public affairs work with each PAO and also served as an adjunct PAO for the reserve center because I lived there.

Life was very good in SACLANT. I was drilling at home, getting paid well, taking training trips to Norfolk, Washington, D.C., and other destinations. I had orders to the NATO school in Oberammergau, Germany, but the admin gods struck and the course was canceled. I could have stayed on cruise control for the rest of my reserve career and would have been very happy.

During this time my official designation, since I was not qualified as a surface warfare officer, was general line officer or 1105. Aviators were 1300s. The "05" designated a reservist. The Navy is always reinventing itself and someone is always tinkering with the reserves. The growing presence of women in the reserve force because they couldn't become warfare qualified created a challenge of what designation the non-combat officers would get.

The Navy came up with Fleet Support Officer, 1705 designator, a vague reserve career field that seemed to be created specifically for women, although officially it was gender neutral. It was later changed to human resources officer and became a viable career path. The first three admirals in that specialty were all women. As a result of my lack of warfare qualification, I was designated a 1705. And, no, it didn't bother me. I was happy doing what I was doing in SACLANT.

Eventually, Capt. Rick Strutner took command of the unit. He lived in South Bend, was a huge Notre Dame fan and operated Goodwill Industries in northern Indiana. Not long after he took command, he sat me down and questioned me about my goals in the reserve. I had potentially 10 years of service left and he was alarmed that I had homesteaded in SACLANT for so long. He was blunt about the fact that the 1705 designation wouldn't get me ahead or promoted in the Navy. He told me I needed to keep moving forward, insisting that I shouldn't stay in SACLANT. He offered to support whatever direction I wanted to go.

He knew I did a lot of public affairs work and questioned why I wasn't in that field. I told him I wasn't warfare qualified and my understanding was that you needed to have a warfare qualification to laterally transfer. He admitted he didn't know a lot about public affairs, but knew that many of them are direct commissioned officers with no warfare skills. He told me I should start looking at public affairs and see what I could do.

This motivated me as I had failed to see that my reservist career had become stagnant. I enjoyed serving in SACLANT and was literally "fat, dumb and happy" with what I was doing, but it took a leader to kick my ass and get me out of my comfort zone.

Through the PAOs in SACLANT, one of whom was Capt. Ken Beachler who was from Lansing and recruited me to the unit, I started finding out who was who in the public affairs community and what units were good ones. Beachler and I remain close friends today. The time he was in SACLANT he was the executive director of the Wharton Center for the Arts at Michigan State University and remains active in the arts today.

I contacted a mutual friend and colleague of his in Milwaukee and made arrangements to drill for a weekend with the public affairs unit there. Capt. Tom Plantenberg, a legend in the public affairs community, was the unit's skipper. My weekend in Milwaukee opened my eyes to the broader scope of the Navy Reserve and the public affairs community. The reserve center in Milwaukee was a straight shot across from Coast Guard headquarters in Lake Michigan and near the water-front. It was a dynamic place to drill. I found out that many reservists at Milwau-kee, including the master chief, worked for Harley-Davidson in civilian life. The Milwaukee reservists were fiercely proud of their town and center's reputation.

The next month, I put together a package detailing my background and qualifications for public affairs and a request to transfer. Strutner endorsed it and sent it up the chain of command. A few weeks later, I was elated when I received a letter informing me that I was reviewed and accepted and now desig-nated a *Special Duty, Public Affairs Officer/1605*. I found a billet at Great Lakes, Illinois, with Navy Information Bureau, Det. 613, with help of the SACLANT PAO. My public affairs career was underway. My only regret was that I hadn't done it sooner.

A Lesson in Organizational Dynamics

In most active duty jobs, personnel come and go, but reservists tend to stay with one assignment longer and many times become a valuable resource for their active duty ship or station.

The same is true for Navy Reserve centers. Most of us who drilled at a particular center tended to stay a long time. We might change units within the center, but generally reservists drill close to home and become a permanent part of the center. Reservists see many commanders come and go. Those who serve as commanders of reserve centers are part of an administrative community called TAR Officers (Training and Administration of Reserves). Many have transferred from other specialties and most take this career path to be with their families, away from the fleet, and live a semblance of a normal life.

As a reservist associated with a center, command changes are frequent. Some TAR officers are very good and have a great relationship with the unit commanders. Others came into the community because they had no other option.

Immediately after Desert Storm, a new skipper took over the Battle Creek Reserve Center. Lt. Freddie Jones was a Navy SEAL who apparently saw arduous duty in the first Gulf War. Many of us believed he got this command as a respite tour. He was not a TAR officer, but attended class to learn about the Navy Reserve. His wife was a dentist who graduated from the University of Michigan and they had a lot of family in Michigan. They bought a house in my neighborhood and we became good friends. He bred Labrador Retrievers and my Zap was one of his dogs.

Knowing his shortcomings, Jones did something remarkable – he let his staff do their jobs without interfering.

What happened under his watch was transformative as morale improved exponentially. Jones, an outgoing and free spirit, worked hard to make the center a fun place. He worked well with senior officers and hosted parties on Friday and Saturday nights of drill weekends.

When word got around the Midwest about the change in Battle Creek, officers and sailors begged to transfer there. The center was a fun and progressive place to be, as things were getting done. Under Jones' leadership, the Battle Creek Reserve Center was named best small command in the Midwest region. The center scored its highest readiness standard in every area of measurement and everyone was well taken care of. We fulfilled our Readiness Mission and things got done! We looked forward to drill weekends each month.

The Battle Creek Reserve Center was flying high. It was a great place to be. The wardroom was close and a can-do attitude prevailed.

During his tour in Battle Creek, Jones was promoted to lieutenant commander. Then, he transferred back to the fleet. His replacement was 180 degrees from Jones. He was an uptight surface warfare type who was sent to the reserve center with little chance of promotion.

From day one he began changing everything. Much like my active duty experience, things went from good to bad after a change of command.

On his first drill weekend, he micromanaged the morning muster. He literally counted sailors, challenging a senior enlisted officer's accuracy. He then changed everyone's working spaces. For the next few drills, we had to move files and set up shop in new spaces. None of us had a choice. But the worst thing he did, in my opinion, was ripping apart the commanding officer's office.

The office was steeped in history and tradition – its walls adorned with gorgeous wood grain paneling. For nearly 50 years, it had served commanders well. He moved down the hall to a glorified closet and expanded the workspace of the administration office. Fortunately, he didn't stay long and retired before finishing his tour.

The next skipper was a gung-ho Surface warrior. He did a decent job, but was high-strung and quirky. A few years before he arrived, the entire outside of the building had been painted white with blue trim and looked very classy. He had it painted haze gray and added a water line on the building and a hull number *101* – our address. The Marines were sharing our building at the time, so he made the Marine side entrance look like an amphibious dock. If he could have gotten the building underway, he would have!

He hosted the Navy Reserve Association Junior Officer Symposium at our center and that was great. Some of our senior leadership was well connected with NRA and helped bring the annual event to Battle Creek. Despite logistical issues with transportation and accommodations, the symposium was a success and helped the center regain a dynamic reputation. The commander was soon promoted and transferred back to the fleet.

Public Affairs at Last!

After finally landing in what was my original vocational intention in the Navy – public affairs, I began drilling at Great Lakes Naval Station north of Chicago. It worked out well as my sister, Elizabeth, and her family lived in Lake Forest, about five miles south of the base. I stayed with them on drill weekends and didn't have to stay in a hotel or base housing.

I was assigned to Navy Information Bureau, Detachment 613. We taught military leaders how to do interviews and speak intelligently about their commands and missions.

In their civilian lives, many of those in the unit were professionals in fields that enhanced our unit's skills. Consider: Jon Bush who became the English department chair at Western Michigan University; Bill Salvin was a corporate media coach who preps executives for high-level interviews including the CBS "60 Minutes" program. Both reached the rank of captain and are considered bright lights in the Navy's public affairs community. Scott Clark was an advertising executive at Leo Burnett in Chicago. His work group there created the Army's "Army of One" recruiting ad campaign.

I knew about Leo Burnett because it was the ad agency for Kellogg's in

Battle Creek. In fact, Howard List, a family friend, was the advertising manager for Kellogg back in the 1950s. He was close friends with Leo Burnett himself and worked with him to create Tony the Tiger, the cartoon mascot for Kellogg's Frosted Flakes and the agency's most successful character. Burnett helped create Kellogg and Kellogg created Burnett.

I felt like I was serving with eagles and didn't want it to end.

The unit was mostly autonomous of the Navy Reserve Center at Great Lakes. Personnel at the center handled administrative chores, wrote our orders and handled our pay. Otherwise, we were on our own to fulfill our mission.

After about a year, a new skipper came aboard, Capt. Mike Smith, and the unit was left without an executive officer. Apparently the person selected for that job took another one. I seized on the opportunity to volunteer to serve as XO since I had a good grasp of the administrative functions. It was a commander billet and I was a lieutenant commander. I viewed it as career-enhancing, taking on a job at a higher paygrade. But I ended up fighting too many administrative battles and not enough time developing public affairs skills. In hindsight, it may not have helped my career.

Smith lived in Washington, D.C., and flew to Chicago for weekends. Many ranking officers don't want to settle for menial jobs in the reserve and most at that level can afford to travel. Many include work travel with drill weekends. Being that flexible improves your chances of getting great billets and promotions.

I knew a few airline pilots who were former Navy aviators and continued as

The author is front and center for a Wardroom Dining In (officers only, no guests) at the Battle Creek Country Club in 1991. The uniform for the event was Service Dress Yankee, a rarely worn, but authorized, combination of summer whites and dress blues. The officers called the uniforms their "yachting blues."

The author with country music artist Lee Greenwood at the commissioning of the USS Ronald Reagan (CVN 76) in July 2003.

reservists. They had the system down, where they could drill anywhere and had the ability to schedule their layovers to accommodate drilling.

The Chicago public affairs unit worked well together and had many accomplishments. We gained a reputation for our media training and put on seminars around the fleet. We conducted training in Corpus Christi, Norfolk, Annapolis and Washington, D.C., among other places, working with many admirals and senior officers as well as civilian leaders. One weekend we trained senior leaders of the FBI.

Sometimes, we would pose as civilians with no Navy connections when we conducted training. It made it easier to critique senior leaders if they didn't know our rank. At the end of the training, we would reveal we were Navy reservists, often to great surprise of our trainees. It was a source of pride for us – winning over those skeptical about reservists.

Since I joined public affairs later in my career, I had a difficult time competing for promotion with more experienced officers. I failed promotion three times. I always looked for opportunities to serve and grow, but if effort and passion got you promoted, I should have been an admiral. I was up against a system.

As a public affairs officer, you do anything and go anywhere there is a need. In 2003, I had an exciting opportunity to augment the public affairs team in Washington, D.C., working on the commissioning of the USS Ronald Reagan in Norfolk. I requested and got orders to spend a week helping prep for the largest military event since 9/11. It became one of the most spectacular, emotional, and gratifying things I did in the Navy.

As great as that experience was, I was soon slammed by an unexpected call from an administrative officer at Great Lakes. She wanted to know if I planned to go to the Voluntary Training Unit (VTU) or transfer to Individual Ready Reserve (IRR). I told her neither. "I plan to continue drilling with the public affairs unit! Why do you ask?"

Apparently, because I hadn't been promoted, I had to be transferred to unpaid status. I had two choices: stop drilling and sit at home in the IRR and check in annually to verify that I was still alive until I officially retired, or go into an administrative unit, the VTU, and show up and collect drill points, but no pay.

I was furious.

I obviously didn't want to give up the work I was doing and, after much consternation, decided to go into the Voluntary Training Unit (there is nothing voluntary about it!) It allowed me to keep drilling with my unit and shipmates, but report to an administrative unit. On drill weekends, I would check in with the VTU then perform my regular duties with the public affairs unit with the indignity of not getting paid. I did that for a few months, collecting only drill points toward retirement. It was humiliating and frustrating, but I made the best of it.

Eventually, the insanity of traveling to Great Lakes at my own expense to collect a few drill points made me look back to Battle Creek. I decided to transfer to the VTU in Battle Creek and do public affairs work there. It was a good plan. I rejoined my former NATO unit. Its name had changed to Supreme Allied Command Transformation as NATO was undergoing many changes. The mission was changing and there was a lot of work to do in the command.

Fortunately, new CO Capt. Cal Bagby was very close to the reserve coordinator at the home command in Norfolk who recognized my talent and needed a PAO for a training event at the Joint Warfare Center in Stavanger, Norway. He figured out how to get me orders and pay for a five-day duty in Norway. It was awesome.

I led a group of Navy journalists culled from other units around the U.S. to help run the public affairs portion of the exercise. Their duties included playing reporters and training the NATO military on dealing with the press.

Most of the team arrived in Norway a week before me and had a good grasp of what was happening. The team was led by an experienced First Class Navy journalist, Darrell Crandall from Wisconsin. Also on the team was First Class journalist Vance Youmans, a professor from Spokane, Washington. The team knew how to get things done.

When they arrived in Norway, the exercise was in various states of readiness. I learned that the journalist team literally saved the exercise because they spent the pre-exercise scripting the events. They prepared virtual events and then injected them into the computer-based training scenario once the exercise began.

The team also helped prepare the Canadian Public Affairs team, which later would go to Afghanistan to do public affairs work for the first Afghan election after liberation. They did a phenomenal job and worked tirelessly to make the exercise successful. I was blessed to work with such great sailors and consummate professionals.

I had to chuckle because this was so typically NATO: an American team, training a Canadian team, in Norway, to go to Afghanistan! It doesn't get more NATO than that!

My role was to support the team and watch over them as the public affairs officer. They did such a stellar job that I made it my mission to get them all the Joint Service Achievement Medal. It took a few months and a lot of work, but they earned it and all received it. It was a rewarding feeling to know that they were recognized and that it helped them with their careers.

While in Norway, I interviewed key players in the exercise – admirals and generals – and wrote a big story before I left that was featured on the Navy News Network and in several military outlets. I was proud of our accomplishments and to get my byline in the military media.

I returned to Battle Creek with great tales to tell. Although I had been passed over for promotion and was in the VTU, I had hoped my recent stellar performance and glowing fitness reports might have redeemed my career. No such luck. I actually found out by logging in on the hotel computer in the lobby in Norway – no promotion for the final time. I would finish my career without pay for my last few years. It put a black cloud over a great victory and performance in Norway.

I was lucky that I had more than 16 years of service at that point and was in a zone that allowed me to stay until I reached 20 qualifying years in the reserve. I had just over four on active duty, so I ended up with about 24 years of Navy service.

I drilled with the VTU and SACT in Battle Creek for a few more years and continued to serve the unit and the center as a PAO. I enjoyed the camaraderie with everyone at the Battle Creek center, but I reached the point I had to retire.

We had a grand retirement party and I invited many friends from the Battle Creek community, including Joe Schwarz, a member of the 109th Congress at the time, who spoke. We had a second party at Gull Lake. I stayed close to many of the friends and officers for several years and some to this day. I retired as a lieutenant commander and can start collecting my retirement pay at age 60. I'm in no hurry to get it, but it will be a sweet bonus when it comes and worth all the frustration I put into serving.

T.R. Shaw's family joined him the day he retired from the U.S. Navy in October 2005. From left, sister Liz and brother-in-law John Gescheidle, mother Esther M. Shaw, nephew Will Gescheidle, niece Grace Gescheidle, and wife Kathy Shaw.

Lesson Learned

While my time on active duty was challenging and professionally un-productive, the best thing I ever did was stay in the Navy Reserve. It provided me with many more opportunities to serve and do things that those on active duty could never do with their strict career paths and planned progression.

I was given responsibility and jobs that challenged me, but that were manageable. I learned a new way of thinking and acting, but also enjoyed senior officers who were more approachable and more willing to mentor and help. On active duty, everyone is uptight about their career paths and making the next selection board. In the reserve, everyone has jobs outside the military and can bring their expertise, including management skills, to the table. Many officers I worked with were outstanding leaders in their civilian and military lives.

The opportunities to experience other fields and occupations in the Navy are abundant in the reserve and leadership has a good grasp of what juniors must do for success.

In many ways, being an unqualified surface warfare officer allowed me to do most anything in the Reserve. I was the ultimate generalist when it came to Navy positions. There was little in the Reserve I couldn't do.

Leadership eventually saw my ability to communicate and do public affairs work. I was finally pushed to find out about public affairs and encouraged to go in that direction. When I made the right connections and got the right information, it was nirvana. I was finally doing what I originally intended to do in the Navy and the time spent represented the best years of my career.

I **Defied the Immediate** so many times that it gave me a great background for public affairs. In some ways my experiences, successes and failures made me a near perfect public affairs officer because I knew the Navy so well and had been exposed to so many communities and disciplines. I had perspective on the Navy and could tell its story well. In some ways, all the bad things that happened to me prepared me for my ultimate job as a PAO.

Had I gone directly into public affairs, I wouldn't have had the background and fleet experiences I needed to be successful.

Moments of failure can be powerful learning experiences and they go into making you, well, YOU!

CHAPTER 13

———

Dealing with Diabetes

"When I work, a lot of times I have to lose weight, and I do that, but in my regular life I was not eating right, and I was not getting enough exercise. But by the nature of my diet and that lifestyle – boom! The end result was high blood sugars that reach the levels where it becomes Type 2 diabetes. I share that with a gajillion other people."

– Tom Hanks

As most of our country evolved over the past half century from an agrarian to a suburban culture where all the food we needed came from the supermarket and not from our gardens, our waistlines grew. We are now paying the price for all that quick, convenient and tasty food with obesity, heart disease and, especially, diabetes.

I'm no exception.

For about 20 years, I've been a Type 2 diabetic. My first exposure to the chronic disease came from relatives and friends who had "sugar," as it was called. A family friend, Harriet Lindaur, who worked for the funeral home part-time and often babysat for my sister and me, had a terrible time with the disease. She had been a Type 1 diabetic since childhood. On many occasions we found her in a diabetic coma where she appeared drunk, drooling and babbling. It scared the daylights out of us kids. Fortunately, another employee, Carl Steele, was also diabetic and knew how to get her back on track with orange juice and honey. As a child, I accepted it as a problem of age because so many older people I knew had it. I never thought much more about it.

In college, diets can go off the rails. Many incoming college students living in dorms and fed in all-you-can-eat cafeterias experience the "Freshmen 15" weight gain. The villain, besides our own lack of willpower, is mostly starchy, high-calorie and sweet food. Without adult supervision, it's a tempting environment for gluttony. For some, it's more than gaining a few pounds. A new lifestyle of classwork, study and eating takes its toll as you are no longer that active kid who was involved in everything. The health risks manifest themselves later in life.

I made it through college in pretty good shape. By my junior and senior year, I was living off campus. I was eating less, because I had to pay for it and was running and working out. I wanted to be in good shape when I entered the Navy. I attended campus Weight Watchers one semester. It was a great place to meet women! I lost about 20 pounds and by my senior year was in the best shape of my life and ready to take on military life.

When I got to Navy Officer Candidate School, it was like being a freshman again. The military, to boost morale, has great food! I found myself eating way too much in the cafeteria again, but the intense course work, physical demands and group PT offset any dietary indiscretions. I left OCS fit, thin and ready to make my way in the fleet.

My first ship, the aircraft carrier USS Dwight D. Eisenhower, was enormous and relatively new. I wish Fitbits had been available then, as I routinely walked several miles each day moving aboard ship in addition to scrambling up and down ladders. It didn't take the Eisenhower long to become renowned for its food service, often earning the Ney Award as the Navy's top culinary ship. With a crew of more than 4,000 when fully embarked, food service was an awesome undertaking.

Officers, me included, ate in the wardroom and the best cooks on the ship worked our kitchen. The food was exceptional and plentiful. I seldom missed a meal and food was available 24/7. Many sailors would grab a slider or hamburger before going on a night watch – the fourth meal of the day.

During the mid-watch from midnight to 4 a.m., stewards would deliver a sheet of warm, fresh pecan rolls to the bridge and combat information center. It was one of the rewards for giving up sleep. They were as delicious as they were calorie-laden.

Potatoes in many forms were at every meal, too. Hash browns at breakfast, French fries at lunch and mashed potatoes with gravy at dinner. It was a carbo-junkie's paradise.

When we got to ports in the Mediterranean, we'd bring fresh local produce aboard, so it wasn't all bad food. One of my favorite memories is blood oranges from Crete. I couldn't get enough of them. When you cut one in half, it was a vibrant red and was the sweetest, tastiest orange ever. I always grabbed a few and took them to my stateroom.

No surprise – I gained weight on IKE. You work long, hard hours and don't exercise like you should. At that time, it was not as critical as it is today in the fleet. In hindsight, I likely would have felt better and performed better had I exercised more and eaten less. But I was still young and indestructible.

After I left active duty, my life changed again. My military career continued on drill weekends in the Navy Reserve but I returned to college at Wayne State University to study mortuary science and live in Detroit.

Our class spent many lunch hours in Detroit's Greektown eating heavy Greek food and pizza. We frequented the Parthenon, Pizza Papalis and other excellent Greek restaurants. During my Detroit sojourn, I also was introduced to the Polish pastry paczki, a traditional treat made just before Lent to use up all the sugar, butter and lard in the kitchen. The confection has grown in popularity and is loaded with everything nobody should really eat. For a few weeks, paczki filled our break room.

After completing my studies in Detroit and returning home to work in the family business, I began the active life of a funeral director. I was on-call 24/7 and worked a crazy schedule, often running between late nights, arrangements and funerals. I'd squeeze in personal time whenever possible. Unfortunately, my own time meant inactive time. I found that the demands of the business made me complacent about my physical well-being. Eating was problematic, too. I'd grab what I could between doing other things. Often it was fast food. Most evenings, I crashed in my easy chair for a few hours until the phone would ring and duty called.

I managed to stay as active as I could throughout this time and was subject to the Navy's semi-annual Physical Readiness Test or PRT. Twice a year you had to take the test to determine your level of fitness. The program evolved during my tenure as a reservist. The Navy and the Navy Reserve changed to place far greater emphasis on physical fitness. I applauded the move.

The test began with a body fat measurement, which I never had a problem with – at first. Once you got measured you had to do the physical portion if you measured below 25 percent body fat. Even if you exceeded the percentage, you could still take the PRT and would be considered acceptable.

Later in my career, the Navy again changed the rules. Body fat exceeding the standard was considered a PRT failure. Three failures and you would be discharged. It wasn't a problem for me until later in my reserve career.

The physical test offered the choice of a 1.5-mile run or a 500-yard swim. I often chose to swim, as I was a much stronger swimmer than runner and I reasoned 500 yards is much shorter than a mile and half. Your time on the run or the swim went into a score. You were also tested on how many sit-ups you could do in two minutes and how many push-ups in two minutes. The results went into a formula that produced one of six classifications: OUTSTANDING, EXCEL-LENT, GOOD, SATISFACTORY, PROBATIONARY and FAIL.

Initially, there was no consequence or reward for SAT or OUTSTAND-ING, so many were happy to meet minimum requirements. Later, they made your score part of your fitness report for officers and evaluation for enlisted personnel and it began to matter. The really good athletes and runners laughed at the easy standard. A 1.5-mile run was a warmup for some of them.

The Navy ultimately cranked up the standards and consequences of failure. My civilian work and lifestyle and part-time reserve duty clashed. Working long hard hours in the funeral business, I found it difficult to keep up with a physical training regime. I got lazy in my 30s. It's especially difficult when you are no longer immersed in an environment that demanded fitness. You had to be self-disciplined to stay fit and avoid PRT fails.

In my late 30s and early 40s. I was always borderline with my body fat measurement, thanks to some generous corpsmen who pulled the tape snugly when they measured me. Failing body fat measurement was now a total PRT failure even if you could achieve an Outstanding on the physical. Now it was three strikes and you were out.

It must have been fate. My once indestructible body was starting to show signs of slowing down as I aged. My epiphany came during a NATO exercise in Norfolk.

I was still fairly new in the NATO Reserve Unit. I needed to get time in at the home command in Norfolk and stand watches in the Strategic Direction Center or SDC. I found an opportunity to monitor an exercise taking place in the Atlantic and get some needed qualifications.

I went to Norfolk in the dead of a cold Michigan winter for a four-day weekend, Thursday to Sunday. I once had lived in Norfolk and experienced Tidewater winters, which were generally wet, rainy, windy and miserable. The February the exercise occurred was no exception.

While standing watch I became extremely thirsty one day and started making constant runs to the drinking fountain to fill my coffee mug and quench my thirst. I blamed my thirst on the change in climate in Norfolk, coming from a cold winter in Michigan.

Through the watch I kept drinking water and making runs to the bathroom. I couldn't quench my thirst. That evening I stopped at the 7-Eleven next to my hotel and picked up two large bottles of Gatorade. I chugged one in a few minutes before going to bed and drank the other throughout the night.

That Saturday night I couldn't sleep for more than 20 minutes without going to the bathroom and then drinking more water. (I had drunk all the Gatorade.) I didn't know it, but my blood sugar was dangerously high.

The thought of diabetes crossed my mind, but I blamed my thirst on the weather and climate change. Besides, I was too healthy to get that old person's disease.

Sitting at the airport that Sunday waiting for my flight home, I couldn't order Cokes quick enough. My thirst was making me crazy. I couldn't wait to get home to a more customary climate.

In Michigan I went to work Monday. Still somewhat thirsty, but being back in my environment it was manageable. I noticed my eyesight seemed a little off, but it had been a long time since I had my eyes checked. I probably needed new glasses, so I made an appointment and got right in. After seeing such a dramatic change in my vision, the optometrist suggested I see my physician. She suspected diabetes, but in my stubborn way, I said I doubted it. I'd been under some stress, spent time in a different climate and I didn't have diabetes. She insisted and even set up an appointment.

My doctor called me that afternoon and told me to go to the hospital immediately. I said I didn't need to, but he demanded that I check in. *"That's crazy, what in the world do I need to go to the hospital for?"* I thought. *"I'm not sick."* Finally, he told me I needed tests. So, I went.

At the hospital, I was handed a gown and assigned to a room. I didn't put the gown on because I didn't think I'd be there that long, all the while grumbling about what the hell I was doing there. *"Can't they do tests at the lab? Why do I need to take up a hospital bed?"* Someone came in and told me to put the gown on and defiantly I did.

"OK, so I'm spending the night at the hospital. I'll go along with all this. Hope this doesn't take long," I thought.

The next morning Dr. Mehmet Yilmaz, my internist, came in and told me that I had diabetes. In my mind, I'm saying *"No, I don't!"* He proceeded to show me my numbers, which at the time meant nothing to me, but now that I know, they were dangerously high. Had I not gone to the hospital, very bad things could have happened to me over the next few days.

I politely listened to what he had to say and what I needed to do, but I was privately defiant. A nutritionist came in and went over diet with me. It went in one ear and out the other. I couldn't have diabetes; I had just had an episode from drinking too much Gatorade!

I was given oral medications, which I took, but still was in denial. I reasoned that I was a little hyperglycemic and just needed to watch myself. I went back to life as usual, refusing to believe that I had a chronic disease requiring my complete attention.

I randomly used the glucometer they gave me, usually only when I was feeling funny. Besides, the test strips were expensive and only gave me bad results. My denial lasted maybe two years.

My doctor appointments usually resulted in an ass chewing, not unlike those I got in the Navy.

My denial finally ended when the doctor showed me my renal protein numbers. They were off the chart staggering. My kidneys were starting to fail and I needed to aggressively change my lifestyle. Kidney dialysis was in my future if I didn't, the doctor said. He started me on insulin and it scared the daylights out of me. I now have to take one or more daily shots, something I really didn't want to do because I feared I could never get off them.

It was about this time that I was starting to struggle with passing the Navy's PRT. Ultimately I had three failures and had to be discharged. My last failure came from the swim. We used the therapy pool at the VA Hospital for the test and the pool was so hot that I couldn't complete the swim. You literally couldn't breathe in the pool area, but the diabetes played a role. Halfway through, I gave up – too tired to finish.

The Navy offered a medical continuation board because I was one of the first to be processed under this new directive. I got help from a JAG officer friend, Commander Dan Downing, who represented me at the medical board. The board was at Great Lakes and adjudicated by a Navy medical officer, a Navy nurse and the Readiness Command chief of staff. I couldn't understand the chief of staff being on it. He is charged with backing and supporting the policy and standing up for the Navy. He had no choice but to vote against me. By a 2-1 vote, I was offered continuation in the Navy Reserve and restored to drilling status.

I had to spill my guts about my diabetes to the board and the personal struggle I was having with the disease. I rarely talked about it to anyone. It was humbling and somewhat humiliating. I was never forthcoming about my condition to the Navy corpsmen at the reserve center for fear it would jeopardize my career.

The board helped me realize that I needed to take control of my disease. And, for a few years, I did.

But as I grew older, the PRT became harder for me and I had a few close calls passing. Eventually, I had three failures again, but the good thing was that I now had enough time in service, over 16 years, so I could stay, in a non-pay status, until I reached 20 qualifying years to retire. The failures prevented me from being promoted and failure to promote is also a reason to discharge.

However, it was at this time that my Navy public affairs career was soaring. I loved everything I was doing for, and with, the Navy. I had found my niche and my working career in the Navy was in high gear.

I retired in October 2005 with a helluva great ceremony and 24 remarkable years I don't regret for a moment. Would I have done things differently? Well, hindsight is always 20/20.

A few years after I retired my diabetes control slipped again. I sat down with my new internist, Dr. Mehmet Ismailoglu, and he told me that I had maxed out on medication and needed to do something radical. He suggested I visit a diabetes specialist at Borgess Hospital in Kalamazoo and I did.

Dr. Mike Valitutto is an excellent doctor, endocrinologist, and rising star in the diabetes world. He is head of the Borgess Diabetes Center in Kalamazoo and an expert at helping diabetics control their disease and their lives – physically and mentally.

An interesting aspect of his practice is group or shared appointments. It was fascinating sitting with other diabetics and hearing them describe their fight with the same disease I was battling.

Some were frightened and facing the reality of their diagnosis for the first time. Other longtime diabetics shared inspiring success stories, which gave renewed hope to those new to the challenge. Personally, though I had been diagnosed years earlier, I found much of what I heard helpful and educational.

Dr. Valitutto's entire staff was very helpful and empathetic. His physicians' assistants follow up with patients. The staff helps the patients understand their cravings and what to do about them.

I consider myself blessed to have found this doctor and his staff. I've come a long ways from my days of denial.

As you age, I've found, everything is more challenging.

Fortunately, we are living in an era in which new drugs and treatments appear almost daily. Years ago, a diabetic didn't have choices in insulin and sometimes the patient himself had to mix it properly.

Today, many diabetics, me included, carry convenient pens that can discretely deliver a needed injection.

Self-monitoring techniques and devices are exploding, new glucometers are coming on the market regularly and the price of testing supplies is falling. My glucometer has a USB port, allowing me to link it to my computer and make printouts of my results or email them to my doctor.

A sensor is imbedded in my arm. I can swipe it with a meter or my phone many times a day for an instant reading of my blood sugar levels and to track daily trends. The advances have made self-care much easier. You don't have to poke your fingers anymore!

Many people today who have a very serious diabetes problem, especially Type 1 diabetics, have a portable, discrete pump to monitor blood sugar levels and inject insulin as needed without even thinking about it. We are very fortunate.

In a stroke of good luck, I came across an ad in the Rotarian magazine for the many Rotarian Action Groups members can join online and be part of a community of interests. I joined the Rotarian Action Group for Diabetes, RAG-D. A few weeks later I was contacted by a board member of the RAG-D. In addition to being a member of the Rotary Club of Chicago, she was the

American Diabetes Association development officer for Michigan and Illinois. She invited me to an ADA event at the University of Michigan. Kathy and I went to the Ann Arbor event and toured the diabetes research labs. One was the diabetic retinopathy lab at the Kellogg Eye Center.

A panel discussion led by top researchers at U-M and the medical director of the ADA highlighted the seriousness of this disease and advances in treatment. I learned that one in three Americans will be diabetic by 2025 and federal funding for research ranks a distant third behind cancer and AIDS research.

Lesson Learned

If you're struggling with diabetes, take heart, you're not alone. In denial as I once was? Get over it. The sooner the better! It's easier than you think and there is a wealth of information, support and help available.

I once lulled myself into the notion that this is not a serious disease. It is deadly serious! Fortunately, it's a controllable medical condition.

I grew up around people with "sugar" and believed it could never happen to me. For the longest time I blamed myself, careless eating habits and lifestyle, and was in total denial. It can be depressing if you dwell on it. But once you get over that hump, it's much easier to control.

Fortunately, researchers regularly develop new pharmaceuticals that offer greater effectiveness and ease of use. Someday, a cure or vaccine to stop or prevent diabetes may be developed. I pray for that day.

Overcoming the mental and emotional challenges of diabetes may be the hardest part. But as your understanding of the disease improves, you'll realize you have the power to control the damage done by this menace. My diabetes was a huge factor in ending my military career.

Don't deny, don't ignore! Do what you must to beat it! **Defy it!**

For more useful information visit the American Diabetes Association website at www.diabetes.org.

CHAPTER 14

It's All in the Family

"The only rock I know that stays steady, the only institution I know that works, is the family."
– Lee Iacocca, legendary automotive company executive

After I left active duty Navy in the spring of 1987 and returned to Michigan, I spent a summer contemplating my future. I interviewed with acquaintances I knew in the public relations field but didn't have a firm grasp of what I wanted to do. I only had my college experience and some public affairs work in the Navy on my resume at that point. It wasn't enough to get a yawn from the people I talked with. Most of them had a bleak outlook for the PR job market. I didn't want to be a reporter and I worked part-time at the family-owned Shaw Funeral Home.

My dad was in negotiations with our colleague and competitor, Don Estes, who owned the Farley-Estes Funeral Home, another 100-year old landmark in Battle Creek. Estes owned property on the south side of town and had plans for it.

Our two downtown funeral homes were separated only by the Presbyterian Church for more than 50 years. At the time, I wasn't interested in the business, but my father always kept the door open for me. He and Estes negotiated a joint operating agreement and partnership to build the Shaw-Estes Funeral Home on Estes's property near the rapidly growing I-94 corridor. My dad would run it and Farley-Estes would offer families the choice of using either facility.

I had occasionally considered going into the funeral business, but my experience while growing up inside and working for the chapel hadn't convinced me. Dad never pushed me, but as I kept looking for work we chatted about what I might do. One night around the kitchen table, he told me he didn't want me to go into the business just because I'd be a fourth-generation of the business founded by my great-grandfather, Franklin E. Shaw Sr. in 1909. I was welcome, but he told me flat out that it wouldn't be easy. And I would have to go to mortuary school and get my license. I thought about it more and looked into mortuary school at Wayne State University in Detroit. It was one of the only schools preparing students in mortuary science that were affiliated with a major university.

Franklin E. Shaw Jr., the author's grandfather; J. Michael Shaw, the author's uncle; Thomas R. Shaw, the author's father, and the author at age 2 attending Father-Son Day at the Battle Creek Rotary Club in 1962. This is the only known photo of three generations of Shaw funeral directors. (Photo by George Vallillee, Battle Creek ENQUIRER)

What really changed my mind was a conversation with our stockbroker and family friend Dave Melges. He handled our family's financial affairs for many years and his father, Dr. Fred Melges, was the leading obstetrician in Battle Creek. Before he retired, Dr. Fred delivered nearly the entire population of the city, including me and my family.

Dave quizzed me on my career plan now that I was out of the Navy. I told him I wasn't sure; that I was staying in the Navy Reserve and thinking about joining the family business. He had insight into where the nation's economy was headed. We had a frank discussion on the merits of family businesses and he told me that the funeral business would be the financially smart thing to do. He thought, rightfully so, that the job market was soft and that I ought to find a vocation and workplace with financial stability. He was right, and I soon began to get serious about training to become a funeral director.

I applied to Wayne State and had no problem getting in. I had a college degree already, but needed a few credits in chemistry. I signed up for a summer class in Chem 101 at Western Michigan University in Kalamazoo where I quickly learned that it was harder than I expected. The class covered a week's worth of material in a day. Keeping up was brutal. Add to that, this class was used to weed out students not ready to be chemistry majors. In my first class, a nerdy professor with a pocket pen protector and horn-rimmed glasses came into the classroom and began lecturing. I soon learned that it wasn't chemistry but math as he began writing theoretical chemical equations on the board. He wrote with his right hand and erased with his left hand as he walked in front of the chalkboard. I couldn't keep up. I tried hard, but only lasted a few days and ended up dropping the class. I only needed the credit to satisfy Wayne State and wasn't planning to cure cancer.

It was a little humbling since I already held a degree and had survived five years in the Navy, and all the technical schools I attended. I swallowed my pride and did what I should have done in the first place – I enrolled at Kellogg Community College. The pace was easier, the demands weren't as intense and I got the needed credit for Wayne State. Throughout my funeral career, I never once balanced a quadratic equation in the embalming room. I did, however, gain an appreciation for the math of volumes and concentrations when dealing with embalming fluid. Math is useful when it's relevant.

Fully ready to begin at Wayne State in the fall, I looked forward to going back to school and start working toward a new life. The future looked bright!

A photo believed taken about 1910 features Franklin E. Shaw Sr. at the back of the ambulance the funeral home ran in Battle Creek. The Shaws, like many funeral home owners, operated an ambulance service until the 1950s. The photo was on Washington Street in front of the Kellogg Fieldstone Sanitarium.

Lesson Learned

After returning from the Navy it took a while to figure out my next career move. I was fortunate my parents were patient and also fortunate, I listened to wise advice.

Life is often about seizing opportunities. We had a new funeral home in a growing market, our family reputation was sterling and it would provide solid financial security. My dad wanted to retire in the not-so-distant future, and I could eventually take over a great business. I also reasoned that times were changing and I could bring new and fresh perspective to the business and make it my own. I later learned it was changing far beyond my comfort zone.

It was time to get to work creating my future. I was fired up and ready to conquer the funeral profession. Going back to school would be a challenge, but much easier this time.

I didn't know it then, but in the days and months ahead I would have to **Defy the Immediate** once again with some of the academic, social and logistical challenges I would face. There is no easy path toward a worthy goal.

CHAPTER 15

A Year in Motown

"I see the people in Detroit are very ... they're like a lot of cities, but they're very proud to be from there and they really want to see change and they really want to see good things happen."

— Robert James Ritchie, aka Kid Rock

After I made my decision to attend mortuary school at Wayne State University in downtown Detroit, I had to find a place to live and work while I was going to school. Wayne is an urban commuter school and has little housing for students in graduate programs. WSU's mortuary school refers its students to funeral homes where you can work and live while attending school. I visited several in Detroit's northern suburbs, but wasn't comfortable with a long commute every day.

My dad hooked me up with one of his classmates from the late 1950s, John Reuter, a principal at the highly regarded Charles Verheyden Funeral Home in Grosse Pointe Park. It was close to school and on Mack Avenue, the northeastern border between Grosse Pointe Park and Detroit. The living accommodations at the home were outstanding and I had a roommate, Bruce Betzler, from Kalamazoo. A fellow Sigma Chi brother, we became friends and had a lot of fun together. Bruce's family operated a funeral home in Kalamazoo, but during our time at Verheyden he was pursuing an advertising major at the University of Detroit. That career path didn't pan out for him. He eventually went to mortuary school, and worked at his family funeral home.

We shared the apartment of the former funeral home manager, Clayton Alandt. Alandt and his wife raised three children in that small apartment. One of them married into the Ford family of automotive fame.

Charlie Verheyden was a legend in Detroit and the funeral business. He died in 1986 at the age of 96, but the stories about him lived on in the staff.

He served the upper crust of Detroit for many years and took care of many of Detroit's other legends, especially in the auto industry. For years he owned the only funeral home in the five Grosse Pointes and for a short time did more than 1,000 funerals a year out of one location. He was a driving force in the Pointes and had his share of controversies with local officials.

When he started in business in the 1920s, parking lots were prohibited in Grosse Pointe Park. He used the backyard for parking, ultimately putting down gravel and then pavement. He fought city hall and the officials eventually relented and allowed parking lots since personal automobiles were becoming more common.

In the 1960s Verheyden built what remains today a state-of-the-art embalming room. It's like a hospital lab in the basement and extends under the adjacent street. It has plumbing for remote embalming fluid machines that pump fluid directly to the tables, reducing fumes inhaled by the embalmer. It remains today the standard of embalming rooms and is frequently visited by mortuary school students and others who hope to duplicate some of it.

I learned from living in Detroit of the rich and diverse ethnic heritage of its residents. There were large enclaves of European immigrants such as Poles, Italians, Greeks, Armenians, Croats, Hungarians and Belgians. Verheyden was a Belgian and built the funeral home adjacent to the largest Belgian neighborhood in Detroit. The Cadieux Cafe, only about a mile away and just off Mack, remains a landmark and was a popular destination for my classmates and me. The bar and restaurant are famous for their mussel dinners and, even more so, for the café's two feather bowling lanes. The traditional Belgian sport is much like bocce ball, except that it's played in an elliptical lane about two feet deeper in the middle than on the sides. The goal is to roll a round flattened disc (think of a full round of cheese) as close as possible to the feather. I never fully understood it, but, hey, I'm not Belgian.

Charlie Verheyden made a fortune in the golden age of funeral service but he didn't believe in insurance. Following a fire one year at the funeral home, he paid cash to restore it and was back in business within days.

One of my favorite stories about Verheyden, who never married and lived at the funeral home his entire life, was his role during Prohibition, the period from 1920 to 1933 when the 18th Amendment to the U.S. Constitution banned the manufacture and sale of liquor.

Prohibition was a joke in Detroit as the flow of booze from Windsor, Canada, across the Detroit River made Detroit the "wettest" town in America.

As the legend goes, Verheyden regularly took his hearse to Canada, filled it up with various liquor and spirits and returned to the U.S. without incident. Who knows, maybe he slipped the booze into a casket inside the hearse. Being Catholic, he entertained Detroit priests in his apartment speakeasy and, in turn, they kept sending parishioners to his funeral home. He became the dominant Catholic funeral home in Detroit for years. His business grew exponentially during Prohibition, but nobody I met seemed to know if he profited from it in other ways.

Verheyden left his fortune, which included homes and dozens of horses in California, to his staff. His staff remained faithful to the end, but his death created a legal nightmare. Nobody seemed to know the extent of his estate or how it should be divided. I believe there were a few distant relatives in the picture, too.

In his final years, he apparently became absentminded and made many confusing changes to his estate papers. An endless stream of lawyers came through the funeral home while I was there. The principals of the business worked well into their 80s because they didn't want to lose out if they retired. A few died before it was ever fully resolved.

In Battle Creek, we knew people who were Dutch, Irish, Italian and of other heritage but we never viewed them as separate parts of a community. In Detroit, ethnic pride remains strong. When Verheyden had a funeral for an Italian person, most of the mourners were Italians themselves and some even spoke in their native tongue.

In the second-floor apartment above the funeral home, I answered the phone at night. All I had to do was call the removal service and they would pick up the deceased. I left notes for the morning crew before leaving for school the next morning. Curiously, at night the phone didn't ring in the apartment, but it set off a bell in the bedroom and I'd have to go to the kitchen to answer. It was sort of quirky and old school.

One night I took a call from Joseph Cappy, a Chrysler vice president and former CEO of American Motors. His wife had died. Dozens and dozens of Chrysler minivans were part of the funeral procession. Another service I recall was for the wife of Mort Crim, then the respected news anchor for WDIV-TV (Channel 4). The entire station staff came to the service and I met many of the Detroit media people. Although I was just a greeter at the front door that evening, Crim was engaging with me. Another memorable funeral was Edith Dossin, the benefactor of the Dossin Great Lakes Museum on Belle Isle.

Not only the directors but most of the part-time staff had worked at Verheyden for many years. An older gentleman who came in overnight and washed the funeral home cars had been there for decades. An elderly cleaning lady came in at 5 a.m. every day. She was afraid of her own shadow and turned on every light in the place before running the vacuum. The only problem was, they never gave her a key. At 5 a.m. every day, the doorbell would ring and I'd have to go down and let her in. One day, I took a garage door opener to bed with me and when she rang the bell, I opened the garage door next to the access door. It scared her and she went home and didn't return until later. I got in trouble, but I think they gave her a key after that.

Verheyden also hired two retired autoworkers for security during visitations and services. They wore coats and had a presence near the door and parking lot. One time I got in trouble because I asked the security guys to help me load flowers into a car. That wasn't their job and I heard about it later. We figured Charlie owed them something and gave them lifelong employment. Charlie left a lot of mysteries behind.

Wayne State's mortuary school was in an old building on West Alexandrine Street off Woodward – a neighborhood that had seen better days. For our own safety, we had to be out of the building by 5 p.m. and we couldn't be there after dark.

On the first day of class, I hadn't moved into Verheyden yet and left from Battle Creek early in the morning. I drank lots of coffee on the way and was wired when I got to class. The first day was mostly administrative, but they did assign us to embalming squads, usually four or five students to a team. One of our instructors, Jerry Cavellier, a funeral director and an instructor for many years, gave us a form to fill out. His goal was to assign us to squads based on who you might be commuting with as everyone came to school from different areas of Detroit and its suburbs.

On his questionnaire, he asked: "Who will you be riding in with?"

I didn't know anyone in the class and would likely be driving in on my own. High on a caffeine buzz and the two-hour drive, I facetiously answered the question, *"J.P. McCarthy,"* who was the legendary morning host on WJR-AM 760, the Great Voice of the Great Lakes in Detroit those days.

Well, Cavellier didn't make the connection as he went through the papers later that day. In fact, he spent the better part of the afternoon with the WSU registrar trying to find out who this McCarthy kid was. He wasn't on the roster and he couldn't find him anywhere. He finally realized my attempt at humor.

The next day, he commented on the smart-ass who said he would be riding in with J.P. McCarthy. *"Do you know how much time I spent looking for this McCarthy kid?"* he said. Fortunately, he was good-humored and thought it was the funniest thing he'd seen in a long time. Lucky for me! We became friends and colleagues. Cavellier was an avid woodworker and had a cartoon in his office that said, *"When I die, I don't want to be embalmed, I want to be Wolmanized!"*

I didn't know many classmates yet, but we quickly became friends. We spent many lunch hours in Greektown and at excellent restaurants along Woodward Avenue in Detroit. The social aspect of school was fantastic.

Dr. Gordon Rose, who had been at the school when my dad attended, was the school's director. His specialty was bacteriology and he was also an expert in biochemistry. He had worked as a funeral home director a few years before going into research and teaching. Dr. Rose had a colorful, to say the least, grasp of terminology. Scientific and complex words rolled off his tongue and he could make the most disgusting things sound romantic. We loved listening to him.

One of his patented creations was a concentrated disinfectant called Brodspec-256. The concentrated sterilant could be diluted in a 1:256 ratio. Half an ounce of it in a gallon of water was a great disinfectant that we used in class and I used for years in my prep room. The product was later sold to one of the chemical companies and renamed. But his students still called it Dr. Rose's Joy Juice.

Dr. Rose, a World War II veteran, was also a colonel in the U.S. Air Force Reserve and served many times as a mortuary officer. He told us about his role on a team in the cleanup and recovery of bodies from the Jonestown mass suicide of 900 members of a California-based cult in Guyana. He was one of the supervising mortuary officers. He talked about the heat in the South American nation and the conditions the National Guard team faced. He said it was the grimmest thing he's ever done or seen. He personally processed the body of cult leader Jim Jones, who had directed his followers, including about 300 age 17 or younger, to take their own lives. He told us when they stripped Jones down, he was wearing a sock in his shorts to make himself more manly.

Our class bonded and became great colleagues as professionals after graduation. Our year at Wayne State flew by. Graduation was always held a few days before the Michigan Funeral Directors Association convention where we all had a chance to let loose and network. Many of us still had to complete our residency and sit for state and national boards to earn our licenses, but most of

Lesson Learned

I was lucky to be somewhat older and more mature than many classmates at Wayne State. My military experience made me organized and focused. I found the academics challenging and stimulating and I was proud to finish my year near the top of my class. I struggled a little with chemistry, but excelled at every other aspect of the curriculum. It left me eager to begin my funeral service career.

I **Defied the Immediate** by working with others toward a goal, overcoming my anxieties and making long-term professional friendships. I grew in many ways. I learned to find my way around and came to love Detroit at a time when the city was struggling.

Working for a quirky, old-fashioned funeral home was great learning experience, but I learned much about the service ethic at Verheyden as well as traditions. We served many cultures and ethnicities.

I was ready to go home and help lead my family business into the future with great confidence. Wayne State prepared me well to be a leader in the profession.

CHAPTER 16

—

Our Family Serving Yours

"Cherish your human connections: your relationships with friends and family."
— Former First Lady Barbara Bush

I went into the funeral business for all the right reasons. I wanted to keep the high standards my family had set for our community. Just as important, I wanted to be engaged in community service, which has always been a hallmark of funeral service.

After graduating from mortuary school and getting my license, I hit the ground running as a funeral director. I had fire in my belly; we had a new funeral home and a new market to develop on the south side of Battle Creek. I was up for the challenge and worked hard at it for a long time. We were very successful.

Almost immediately, I got involved in as many things as I could. I volunteered for boards, joined Jaycees and, later, service clubs such as Rotary and AMBUCS. My participation was also good for my business. People who knew me often would call me in their time of need. My connections brought many new families to our family business. I was often disappointed when someone I knew well, but who had connections with my competitors, didn't call us.

Our new location opened opportunities with many families in rural East Leroy and Athens, my mother's hometown. In fact, we had many good clients in Athens when we moved to our new location; owners of the local funeral home were aging and facing business challenges that resulted in bankruptcy. We became the funeral home of choice for Athens and considered building a new chapel there. In hindsight, we were wise not to make that investment.

For many years I put in a lot of hours, working seven days a week. I did a lot of the embalming and my skills always drew compliments from families happy with the appearance of their loved ones. I was proud to have my work appreciated. It took me a while to get comfortable making arrangements with families. I often sat in with my dad to watch him adeptly handle the tough moments. Once I developed my own style and confidence, I did great, even with difficult families.

One of the first challenging arrangements I handled was with a mother whose son had committed suicide. She was angry. Her son had some hard knocks in life and had threatened suicide several times, leaving her in a constant state of worry. Later, he ended his life. She was mad at the world, and mad at the hospital and doctors. I took the brunt of much of her anger when she came in to make funeral arrangements. The young man's body was not presentable although I did embalm him well so she could have some private closure. We covered his head in the casket and offered to let her come in and at least see his hands. We thought that would ease her pain, but she refused and insisted on a closed casket, unable to bring herself to see him.

She was angry the entire service. This is one of the most uncomfortable things a funeral director has to deal with. We hoped she would eventually see and appreciate all we did for her and her family. She did, and ultimately made pre-arrangements for funerals for both her husband and herself.

Another difficult situation arose when we handled our first service for an AIDS victim. In mortuary school, we were well trained to handle victims of the terrible disease. I knew that the virus doesn't remain alive for long following death. With the proper treatment there is no risk of infection for the embalmer. Embalming, in fact, was the easy part.

The young man who died was in a gay relationship and his father, who made the funeral arrangements, never accepted it. He wanted nothing to do with his gay friends. As far as he was concerned, they had killed him with their sexual contact. He was angry and I had to separate his family and friends at the service. The father was grateful for my efforts and complimentary of our services. Still, the situation was tense and nerve-wracking.

Some of the toughest arrangements occur when the family is indigent or just doesn't want to pay. Some people seemed to think that the state or the VA would pay for their loved ones' funerals. The funeral service business is among few willing to serve people, regardless of their ability to pay. We found ways to make it work, but too many people were trying to get something for nothing. People who had substantial means to take care of a family member and claimed their loved one was in poverty, even if the family wasn't, would infuriate me. We had an old saying that for some families, "Love ended at the checkbook."

There also are many people who have made no contingency plan for death, often leaving the family in financial and emotional chaos. Past generations usually set aside funds, bought insurance and planned for a funeral.

Toward the end of my career, I saw more and more of this. We claimed that the Wal-Mart mentality had entered funeral service. It made me reconsider

The Shaw Funeral Home in downtown Battle Creek where the author, his sister and parents lived on the third floor for 17 years. It was originally the home of industrialist H.B. Sherman and remodeled as a funeral home by the author's grandfather, Franklin E. Shaw Jr., in 1949.

remaining in the business. Fewer and fewer people were appreciating the level of and commitment to service that we provided. We prided ourselves in offering the best, but many opted for a simple cremation with a gathering later on. This went against everything I believed in and worked hard for. The Internet is partly to blame as everyone is now an expert on funeral service and can't discern good advice from poor advice and certainly can't discern quality merchandise online.

While we had many great funerals with very satisfied families, regulation and government involvement was becoming a burden. In Michigan, funeral directors are required to put in a third-party escrow the entire amount they receive for a pre-paid funeral. I took this as a sacred trust when people prepaid. The money was not mine until the time of death. We wrote guaranteed contracts as a matter of principle. We took the risk with investing it, but also reaped the reward if it outperformed the market. We counted on investing the payments to collect enough interest or stock appreciation to match inflation. That was the only way for us to guarantee a funeral in the future at today's cost.

When the economy dipped in 2008, many funeral directors were seeing red with their pre-funded arrangements. Many of our contracts lost not only the gains that offset inflation, but we were losing principal. If a death occurred, we guaranteed the price. We often provided a service and had to show a pre-need discount when we actually lost money. It was a tough time, but those on the ethical high ground dealt with it. The market came back and funds grew again. To put it in perspective, a foundation I served on lost $30 million in 2008. Had it not "held the course," it would never have come back. Pre-need funds eventually came back, but it was a time of great angst. Many funeral directors panicked and switched to less volatile CDs. They lost big time when the market returned.

During this time, suppliers were cutting prices and offering reduced pricing to help offset losses they took on pre-need contacts. One salesman offered us cheap, Chinese-made caskets. His pitch was that they look just like the name-brand caskets and would help cover our pre-need losses. I almost threw him out of the funeral home. First, I'd never let a Chinese casket through my door and, second, I'm not going give families something less than what they paid for even if they'd never know the difference. That was not going to happen on my watch. Many in funeral service jumped on deals like this out of desperation. I saw many abandoning their ethics. The funeral profession was losing the moral high ground. Some cooked the books to circumvent pre-need trust requirements, taking money that wasn't legally theirs. Some got caught and later ended up in jail. It bothered me immensely.

Troublesome families and circumstances were still the exception. It was always refreshing and encouraging when we had families who wanted top-notch services. That's what we were in business for. When you really connected with a family and went the extra mile to earn their confidence and respect, it was worth every hassle you had with others.

I could probably write another book about the things that happened at funerals and in arrangements – some were funny; some were frightening.

Just as important to me as my community involvement was my professional development. Shortly after getting my license, I was asked by the district director of the Michigan Funeral Directors Association to join the district board. I accepted and didn't tell my parents. They were surprised and thrilled to learn about it while attending the district meeting where I was elected in absentia.

I eventually became president of District 3 of the association, which represented all the funeral homes in southwest Michigan. In that role, I ran the district meetings and worked closely with the District 3 director, a funeral home owner who also sat on the state board.

That director was caught using prepaid funeral fees to pay for elaborate trips when he couldn't deliver the services his clients had paid for. He was prosecuted and went to jail.

His misfortune was an opportunity for me: I became District 3 director and proudly joined the association's state board.

As district director, I opened the lines of communication with all the members, corresponding with and contacting them frequently to keep them up to date on the association. I was always annoyed that the only contact I ever had with the previous director was his calls to solicit political contributions. I vowed that I would not be that kind of director, but soon found out that apathy among the membership made my communication efforts mostly one-way. With nearly 50 funeral homes in the district, I rarely received feedback, input, or calls for assistance.

As I became more adept at running the business my mom and dad got away more often, many times to Chicago to see my sister. Her first child, Will, was born in 1999 when they were living in downtown Chicago. A year later they had a career change and moved to suburban Lake Forest and established a food safety business out of their home. They moved at a time when my dad became ill and he never had the chance to spend a night in their new home.

At the Shaw Funeral Home, business was growing along with my confidence in my profession. But in 2001 my dad died and everything changed.

My wife, Kathy, was a huge help with the administrative duties. She organized service folders and did the entry work in our data base in addition to working visitations and funerals. During this time, she also helped care for her aging parents with her two brothers, Durrell and Tim Banfield. Her father Arthur, died four months after mine did.

My mother, Kathy and I worked hard to run the business well, but times were changing, and not for the better. Through this time, my sister Elizabeth was an officer of the corporation, and served as a sounding board for me. We had many serious conversations about the business, along with her husband John Gescheidle.

The long hours were wearing thin. Staying on top of everything was increasingly a challenge and marketplace forces were eroding my profession's stature. Finding and keeping talented associates to help run the home was becoming more difficult. I began contemplating life beyond funeral service.

Lesson Learned

My funeral career began well. A turning point came when I lost my father. I worked hard taking care of business and growing it, but the paradigms were changing. I was realizing that the business wasn't my true passion. I was good at what I was doing, but for the most part was simply going through the motions; my heart was drifting from it.

There comes a time when what you do at one point in your life may not be what you do for the rest of it. I watched as too many funeral directors literally died at the office and never had a life outside the business. I didn't want to go there; I had other things to accomplish. If anything, the turn of events made me think about my future and what was next, especially seeing my dad's death too soon. My dad alluded to the brevity of life and experienced the terminality of life. It was increasingly clear to me that the funeral business was no longer for me.

As a philosopher once said, *"You can always make more money, but you can never make more time."* It was time for me to **Defy the Immediate** and look toward the future once again.

CHAPTER 17

A Father's Passion and a Family's Love: Priceless

"The greatest legacy one can pass on to one's children and grandchildren is not money or other material things accumulated in one's life, but rather a legacy of character and faith."

— Billy Graham

My dad, Thomas R. Shaw, was born in 1935, the middle son of Franklin Jr. and Elizabeth Shaw. Dad, his older brother Frank III (Pete), and his younger brother Mike grew up in a multi-generational household with Frank Jr.'s siblings and their grandmother Cornelia. Frank, Jr.'s younger brother Bill and his sister Margaret (Aunt Peg) also lived there; his brothers John and Bob soon married and moved out. It was a large and close-knit family.

John served in the Army and went on to Albion College. He became a successful insurance agent for many years in Battle Creek. He retired from Mass Mutual, and his son Tim took over his business and clients. Bill enjoyed a career as an ink salesman in Chicago. He became the primary ink salesman to Wrigley and it made him wealthy. For many years all of Wrigley's gum was packaged and sold in wrappers printed with ink sold by Bill Shaw. Peg had a long career in the federal government.

The big house they all lived in was on Ann Avenue in the Washington Heights neighborhood of Battle Creek. At the time it was the most fashionable area in town and near the famous Battle Creek Sanitarium, a health spa that attracted visitors from around the country. Its founder, Dr. John Harvey Kellogg, was frequently seen walking or riding his bike and wearing his trademark white suit on the streets of Washington Heights. Many of my relatives remember chatting with him. Credited as the inventor of Corn Flakes, along with his brother Will Keith (W.K.) Kellogg, he was outgoing and charismatic.

Many doctors who worked at the Sanitarium, as well as civic and business leaders lived in Washington Heights.

Frank Jr. began college at the University of Michigan and hoped to have a career in finance. But he left U-M before graduating to take over the family funeral business when his father, Frank Sr., died unexpectedly at age 52. Frank Jr. attended mortuary school in New York and became a licensed funeral director.

Dad told us many stories about growing up in the big house with a large family. His mother, Elizabeth died in 1956 and the family moved to the rapidly growing suburbs south of town. They dubbed their new home "The Annex" when the older children moved out to college and married. Dad was still in high school when they moved, and he graduated from Lakeview High School, as did Mike.

Frank Jr. remarried and later moved to a home on Goguac Lake in Battle Creek as the youngest boys went on to college.

Frank Jr.'s oldest son Pete graduated from U-M. He had a brief stint with the U.S. Coast Guard between his sophomore and junior year in college on the icebreaker Mackinaw (WAGB 83) in the Great Lakes. He then settled into a career as an executive with the Kellogg Company for almost 30 years. After retiring, he worked almost daily with us at the funeral home. Mike, the youngest of Frank Jr.'s three boys, also graduated from U-M, and spent time as a supply officer in the U.S. Navy before his successful accounting career at the Upjohn Company in Kalamazoo. He also worked at the funeral home in retirement.

Dad's path to education was rockier. An Eagle Scout, he followed Pete to Ann Arbor, but found U-M's classes very difficult. He briefly enrolled at nearby Eastern Michigan University, and then enlisted in the U.S. Air Force Reserve. Dad then decided to join his father in the funeral business. He earned his degree in mortuary science at Wayne State University in 1957 and became a licensed funeral director. Dad was the only child or sibling of Frank's who was remotely interested in the funeral home and funeral business. When Dad was still quite young, his father handed him the reins to the business. Frank Jr. never was passionate about the funeral service, having come into it through the tragic circumstances of his father's early death.

Dad had to professionally grow up quickly, and the funeral business became his passion. With my mother as his life and business partner, they truly loved funeral service.

Dad's years with the Shaw Funeral Home began soon after it was established in a remodeled mansion on one of the most gilded streets in Battle Creek. Fifty years earlier, Capital Avenue N.E. was called Maple Street, and the homes were palatial. Many were built by the industrial revolution titans when Battle Creek was a booming manufacturing community. Frank Jr. bought the home of H.B. Sherman in 1949. Sherman was the founder of the H.B. Sherman Manufacturing Company, which made brass fixtures, mostly lawn and garden equipment and attachments. The company developed the famous "walking sprinkler," which I remember using as a child. It was all brass and weighed about 20 pounds, but water pressure propelled it along the hose.

When Dad started at the funeral home in 1958, Frank Jr. had turned over operations to his employees and funeral directors. My dad's arrival brought new challenges for those employees, as well as himself. Being the owner's son is always a challenge, no matter what business it is. I experienced some of that when I started.

Ultimately, some employees who felt professionally threatened left, but Dad managed it with a small crew of loyal full- and part-timers.

The following year, 1959, Dad married my mother, Esther Smith, and she joined him in the business, handling many of the administrative duties. They were a fine team and business grew sharply during the 1960s and '70s as I was growing up. I remember Dad working long hours and often coming home late.

When they were engaged, Mom helped him buy his dream car, a 1959 Alfa-Romeo Giulietta Spider. They drove it to Nantucket for their honeymoon. A year later, I was told I was nearly born in the Alfa as Dad drove Mom to the hospital. The car was damaged in a garage fire in the 1970s and sat for more than 25 years in various states of disrepair. Restoring it was to be one of Dad's retirement projects, but he never made it. After his death, we connected with an Alfa-Romeo expert and had the car fully restored. I was 50 the first time I drove it. Today, it's a priceless part of our family history and will stay that way.

In the 1970s, Mom and Dad sold our home in the suburbs and we moved into the funeral home where we stayed for 17 years. Dad could be close to the business there and spent many nights in his downstairs office catching up on paperwork and preparing for the next day. It wasn't all bad because we were now close enough to walk to school. My parents made a lot of sacrifices for the business, but living in close quarters above the funeral home was a great experience. It also enabled us to afford, fix up, and spend summers at the family cottage on Gull Lake!

Even though he didn't graduate from there, the University of Michigan was one of Dad's passions. His family had been loyal fans of the football team and rarely missed a game. They held season tickets before they were so difficult to get. In fact, Dad became the point man in Battle Creek for U-M football tickets as the brand grew in the 1970s under athletic director Don Canham and coach Bo Schembechler. I answered many calls at the office from people wanting or selling tickets to upcoming games. Dad eagerly brokered tickets and often gave them to people with kids. He would never, under any circumstances, take more than the face value. Scalping was anathema to him.

On many football Saturdays, after I was licensed, Dad would get an 11 a.m. funeral started, turn it over to me, change his clothes in the office and be in his seat in Ann Arbor for a 1 p.m. kickoff. I can neither confirm nor deny whether he broke the speed limit!

Dad, along with close friends Joe Schwarz and Dave Church, organized the M-Day Golf Outing in Battle Creek for many years. The event coincided with Opening Stag Day at the Battle Creek Country Club for years. It began in 1969 with the arrival and introduction of Bo Schembechler and grew until the school reined it in (along with new NCAA Compliance Rules). It ended because bean counters at the school thought it should make more money for U-M, and the coaches and athletic directors had less autonomy to do such events.

Dad was not only passionate about U-M football, but was also greatly engaged in other community events. He became president of the Battle Creek Rotary Club in 1971 and I remember joining him for many of the meetings. In those days the meetings took place in the Hart Hotel in Battle Creek. In the days of slower travel, it was a marquee hotel that hosted many traveling celebrities who showed up at Rotary meetings. I remember Dad telling me about the television cowboy star Roy Rogers stopping in for the meeting.

I also remember going with Dad to the Rotary's annual Father-Son Day and Christmas luncheon for Battle Creek's disabled children. Many were in leg braces or wheelchairs. Polio was still an epidemic then. Many other children were deaf or blind.

Most of the children were students at Ann J. Kellogg Elementary School, which the city's special needs children attended.

I was excited when Dad told me we were going to the Rotary Christmas party, but he didn't tell me that there would be many disabled kids there. At first, I was shocked and wondered, "What's wrong with them?" Dad explained what the party was about and how we should help those less fortunate than us. I realized for the first time that some kids just didn't have it as good as I did. It was an epiphany that not everyone is as healthy and as "normal" as you are. To this day, it is one of the profound learning experiences I have had. Sadly, few Rotarians took their kids to the party. Looking back, society was much different and less accepting then.

We still attend the Rotary Children's Party, but now it's in a bigger venue and involves kids from several elementary schools. Fortunately, only a few now are disabled, but many of them come from poor or dysfunctional homes. We've made strides in the war on childhood disability through research and medicine, but still have a long way to go on poverty. Rotary has been at the forefront of eradicating polio. It's unheard of today. The kids are treated at the party to a good meal, entertainment, a visit from Santa Claus and a bag of donated toys and clothes. For many kids, it's the highlight of their Christmas season. Dad never missed it and was frustrated that more Rotarians didn't get involved or take their own kids.

Dad was also a huge supporter of the Michigan Funeral Directors Association. He rarely missed a district meeting and felt, as professionals, we needed to network to enhance the profession. As a child, I suffered through many of the meetings but when I became a funeral director, I became as enthusiastic about serving the profession as Dad did. He eventually became a district president and earned a seat on the MFDA board representing southwest Michigan, a seat I held nearly 30 years later.

He was selected as MFDA Recording Secretary, the first chair in a multi-year progression to the presidency. He backed out of that commitment, as it was too much to do and came when we were building our new funeral home. I don't think he was really comfortable leading a statewide organization. He preferred to make an impact closer to home. He also feared public speaking, a trait I, fortunately, didn't inherit.

In 1975 after deciding to expand, he saw an opportunity to buy a small funeral home in Bellevue. Longtime funeral director Carl Lehman wanted to retire and was selling his home in the town just north of Battle Creek. We renamed it Shaw Funeral Home, Lehman Chapel. Bellevue is a bedroom community where most residents worked in Battle Creek and many others commuted to Lansing. The town was about halfway between the cities. It had a sizable Catholic population, most of whom were Hungarian families who came to the area to work in the limestone quarries.

Buying the Bellevue funeral home was one of the best business decisions Dad ever made. Many months when things were slow in Battle Creek, Bellevue picked up the slack and kept us in the black.

Lehman was among an older breed of funeral directors who had a second job as a furniture dealer with a storefront downtown. He told stories about being a World War II embalmer in England. They often embalmed 100 bodies a day from the battlefields, mostly with pure formaldehyde. None of today's safety precautions were taken.

In many small towns, funeral home operators had a second business. Like most funeral directors, Lehman had a sense of humor. A sign in his furniture store read, *"Carl Lehman, funeral director and furniture dealer... comfort for the living and the dead!"* In his bedroom above the funeral home, which was across the street from the fire station, he had the switch for the town's fire alarm as he frequently answered the night fire call phone and tripped the alarm alerting volunteer firemen in the community.

Lehman helped us with funerals until his health declined. His wife, Pauline, also joined us at many visitations and funerals.

In the early '80s, Dad wanted to distinguish us from other funeral homes and considered getting an Airstream "Family Funeral Coach" to transport families from the funeral service to the cemetery. The iconic Airstream motor home company manufactured the plush coach. Very few were sold. With seating for 12-15 passengers it had a compartment in the back for a casket. Flowers could be stored near the vehicle's rear end. Dad thought this would be a bold step to serve our client families. It was!

Some people loved it because everyone could sit together in comfort. Others refused to go to the cemetery in what they called a "bus." It had excellent potential for burials far from the funeral service. Others opted for the traditional funeral coach.

Part of what doomed our coach was when we had it as a demo. Dad invited many of his friends to ride in the coach to a U-M football game. He wanted opinions on the concept. Those who went on the coach to the game loved it, so Dad bought it and started marketing it as an exclusive service. But the trips to Ann Arbor gave the family funeral coach a reputation as the party bus. Someone once joked that a beer bottle rolled out from under the seat during a procession. Even so, Dad was proud of it and it definitely set us apart from our competitors.

Over time, however, the Airstream became a maintenance nightmare. Its size meant it couldn't be stored inside. Leaving it outside, it became a challenge to keep clean. Many of us who drove it smashed mailboxes when we backed out of driveways. It was a yacht to drive! Once, I hung it up on the corner of the funeral home when I turned too tightly. We had to have a semi-wrecker come to move it during a funeral. That was not a good day. When the side door opened, steps descended. Dad often turned off the breaker so the steps wouldn't go up and down every time the door opened. Unfortunately, he once drove off with them down and ripped them partially off on a curb. We had to get a hack saw and cut off the steps so we could drive it.

Only one motor home dealer in Michigan could properly service it, and that dealer was in Holland, about a 90-minute drive. We experienced a few break-ins, too, and the coach became a liability. We eventually sold it although many people continued to ask for it. In many ways, Dad was a visionary and risk-taker.

I believe his love for automobiles and everything automotive explained his infatuation with the Airstream. One of my best memories every January was going with him and his childhood friend and my godfather, Dick Stiefel, to the Detroit Auto Show in Cobo Hall. Later known as the North American International Auto Show, it was the premier opportunity for manufacturers to unveil new models. (As an aside, 2019 was the final year the show was held in

January, a decision made as European manufacturers like Porsche, Mercedes, Volvo, Audi and others were skipping the show in favor of larger venues.)

Every year since I was old enough, Dad and I seldom missed a show where we would be among the first to see the new cars. When they appeared on the streets in the spring you could say, "Hey, I saw that at the auto show!"

Since we owned a fleet of funeral home cars, dad focused his attention on the Cadillac display. He asked questions that revealed a keen understanding of the products – something the Cadillac salesmen appreciated. A week or so later after the show, his interest was rewarded with a collection of Cadillac promotional merchandise like hats, shirts and jackets arriving in our mail. By the time I attended the Detroit show as the principal of our business, the Cadillac folks had become far less generous with their gifts. It was frustrating that I could never score the loot dad could with the car people.

Both my dad and my grandfather treated the salesmen who came calling at the funeral home very well. In our trade, many sales people sell specialty products and services. Dad was cordial, even when the salesman was annoying. I remember one in particular who sold specialty promotional items like calendars, pens, gizmos and you name it. He apparently was pretty successful with us because over the years we accumulated matchbooks, smelling salts, kitchen tools, rain bonnets, pens and everything under the sun emblazoned with the words Shaw Funeral Home. Even today, people bring me items they've picked up at garage sales and I have to laugh. I tell them the trinkets are reminders of our regular visits from the world's greatest salesman.

Reversing Roles

In the spring of 2000, Dad went into the hospital for routine abdominal hernia surgery. He recovered in time for our wedding that June. As fall approached, he wasn't feeling well and returned for blood work, not knowing what was wrong with him.

My mother answered the call from Dr. Steve Smiley, the local oncologist, with the devastating news. Smiley perhaps signed more death certificates than any physician in Battle Creek. Odd, but that was my first thought as a funeral director. Anytime someone was under his care, it never seemed to be good news. I never understood how he could mentally handle the fact that so many of his patients didn't survive.

Dad had an aggressive form of non-Hodgkin's lymphoma, which needed immediate and radical treatment. Smiley needed to get him in for chemotherapy as soon as possible. Visibly shaken, Mom began to cry as she told me the news. My heart sank and I cried, too. Life took a dramatic turn for our family.

I had been running the funeral home a lot more since Dad's surgery, in his absence and recovery, and it looked like he wasn't going to be working much in the near future. All we wanted was for him to beat his illness and return to good health. I thought he could. He was strong, a fighter, and in capable hands.

Dad handled chemo well and things were looking up. In follow-ups, his white cell count was rising and the chemo seemed to be working. But it left him tired and unable to do much but relax at home. Around Thanksgiving he was having trouble breathing. An MRI revealed his lungs were rapidly deteriorating as a side effect of the chemotherapy. He was hospitalized, while more tests were done. The tests showed he was rapidly losing lung capacity. We asked about a lung transplant since he was only 65. We were told that with his lymphoma and chemo treatments, a transplant was not an option.

There was little to celebrate at Christmas with dad in the hospital fighting for his life. He was still alert and watched Michigan play Auburn in the 2001 Citrus Bowl. Michigan won 31-28. Shortly after the game, U-M's head coach Lloyd Carr called Dad. It was a wonderful moment for all of us!

A few days later, Dick Stiefel came into the room to visit. Dad was groggy and couldn't speak at the time, but when he saw Dick he grew animated and shook his hand with a double clasp. He wouldn't let go. That sight, one of the most powerful things I saw him do before the hospital staff induced a coma, is forever etched in my memory.

The hope was that the coma would allow him to fully relax so his lungs could recover and rebuild themselves. Dad never came out of the coma, as we kept praying for the best. After two weeks, the doctors agreed there was no longer a possibility of recovery or getting off the respirator. They recommended taking him off the machine and allowing him to die painlessly and quietly.

I would have none of it.

I adamantly refused and they kept him in ICU and on the respirator for a few more days. They knew it was hopeless, but I didn't want to believe it. I believed he was fighting and it was up to us to give him every chance to pull through. I'm not saying I didn't trust the doctors, but I felt he would want us to not give up.

Eventually, the pulmonologist sat us down and showed us how much lung mass he had lost and was still losing. In the face of overwhelming evidence, I relented, and mom and I made the painful decision to let him go.

Our friends, Dr. Joe Schwarz and Dr. John Giradot, checked on him several times a day and were with him to the end. Joe pulled me aside and tried to prepare me. He urged me to get help with the business for the next few days. I had already backed off on work and the staff was running things. Fortunately, it was slow at the funeral home and I didn't have to worry about much.

After about 10 days of agony and angst, it looked like the end was near.

The author with his father, Thomas R. Shaw,, on a family day cruise aboard the USS Dwight D. Eisenhower. His mother also made the trip and the families were treated to an airshow that included an F-14 supersonic flyby.

They slowly removed equipment from the room and things were quiet as his breathing became slow and shallow. He was expected to pass in the early afternoon and we all sat through the agonizing wait. I'd seen death before, but seldom the process of dying.

Earlier in the week there had been a huge snowstorm and as I gazed out the hospital window everything was white. I was lost in thought as mom looked out, too, while John Giradot stood next to the bed monitoring the EKG, about the only device left in the room.

Suddenly, Mom exclaimed, *"Look at that!"* A formation of Canada geese from the open pond across from the hospital took flight, formed a V and came directly toward the window. I jumped up. They looked like they would crash into the window, but at the last second they flew up and over the roof. This was the moment Dad died. It was almost like the geese were his upward escorts.

Dad was 65 on the day he died – Jan. 20, 2001. Joe Schwarz arrived moments later. He was a state senator at the time and had tickets to the first inauguration of George W. Bush on that day. Instead, he stayed home to be with us. That was true friendship and we'll never forget it.

Dad's older brother Pete was there, too. His younger brother Mike brought the van and the cot to remove Dad's body. Both were retired and working for us, which was a blessing. I waited until they came and made phone calls to friends and family. Pete and Mike came in and, teary-eyed, I helped them get Dad's body onto the cot, as I've done throughout my funeral career. I asked a friend, John Gores, to prepare the body. John's funeral home is in Delton, about 20 miles north of Battle Creek. John also conducted the funeral with help from another funeral director and longtime friend, Roy Betzler from Kalamazoo.

What a tremendous and emotional ride that was as the three brothers took one last ride together through the snowy Michigan countryside.

It dawned on me that this was one of the few times in my funeral career that I had witnessed a death. As funeral directors we typically deal with the aftermath of death, but seldom with dying. I took care of my maternal grand-father and witnessed his dying and death, but he was in his 80s and, although emotional, was not that difficult. He'd lived a good, long life.

I had a hard time transitioning from professional to family member. I felt I needed to take charge of the funeral and do the best I could.

Shortly after his death, we contacted Marsellus Casket Company, which was still operated by the Marsellus family in Syracuse, New York. John Marsellus, the company's president, was a good friend and my parents spent lots of time with John and his wife at funeral meetings. Dad and John shared their support and passion for Ducks Unlimited, the non-profit conservation group dedicated to preserving and restoring wetlands and other wildfowl habitat.

John personally had the plant tailor a special mahogany casket for Dad with a beautiful French blue velvet interior and made sure it was delivered promptly. It was a masterpiece.

Despite a heavy snowfall a few days earlier, a huge stream of family, friends, families we had served, community leaders and funeral directors from around the state crowded into the funeral home. I greeted them but regretted not being able to chat as they kept moving through. Mom, my sister and I were over-whelmed.

Dad's visitation and funeral was unique. We put his prized photo of Mich-igan Stadium, the Big House, on the wall over his casket. Maize and blue, the University of Michigan's colors, were everywhere. Dad would have loved it.

The service was at St. Thomas Episcopal Church where four generations of our family had been married and buried. The Rev. Mother Joy Rogers conducted the service. Gores and Betzler ran the service, but beforehand, I had a difficult time remaining in the parlor with our family. I was constantly checking the chapel to make sure everything was right. I was challenged to separate my roles of son from funeral director.

My sister and I spoke at the funeral. Standing at the pulpit and looking at the standing room only crowd in the church was almost overwhelming, but I told some of the stories I've told here, about going to the Auto Show and start-ing funerals and getting to his seat in Ann Arbor before kickoff.

Once the service ended, I was the last one to get into the limousine. Mom had to tell me to get in. I was still trying to help get cars in the procession.

We drove to the cemetery with a police escort arranged by a friend on the city commission.

As soon as the limo stopped I tried to get out, but Mom grabbed my arm and wouldn't let me go. She kept telling me to wait. I felt like a caged squirrel, that I had to get out of the car and do my job. Sitting there was the hardest, most frustrating thing I had to do. I eventually got out and it seemed normal again. Longtime friend and vault supplier E.J. Brutsche and his son Tim were at the grave, making sure the burial went smoothly. It was humbling seeing so many funeral service colleagues and friends help.

Tom Shaw left us with a rich legacy of service and a sterling reputation in the community and profession.

Of the many tributes, none was more touching than the commentary in the St. Phillip Catholic Church bulletin. Rev. Fr. William Fitzgerald, or Father Fitz, as we knew him, was the priest at the Catholic Church and we had handled many funerals with him over the years. He dedicated his weekly column to Dad the week he died. He compared Dad to the Good Samaritan, who quietly went about serving people and doing what needed to be done in the community. The moving tribute hung in a frame at the funeral home until we sold it.

Without Dad, my work was more challenging than ever over the next decade. My wife and I worked hard but the profound changes in society and in the funeral profession ultimately made us reconsider our missions in life. We sold the 106-year-old family business in September 2015.

Dad would have been proud that we kept the business strong and sold it at the top of its game. But the winds of change were blowing and he likely would have done the same. It was bittersweet, but we did the right thing at the right time. Had Dad lived, things would likely have been much different, but his legacy of care and compassion will live forever!

Lesson Learned

We don't always appreciate our parents until we lose them. I was privileged to see my father at work while I grew up living in the funeral home. I saw his good reputation and character in business and community service. I was proud that he stood on the moral side of most discussions I witnessed. He was an Eagle Scout to the end.

Family businesses are tough. My dad took over under difficult circumstances and was considered a great success. The funeral profession was his passion and, in my humble opinion, he was the best in our business. The profession and community lost a titan.

When he was diagnosed with lymphoma, we hoped an aggressive treatment plan and first-class care would help him beat it. We couldn't think in terms of losing him. His condition deteriorated quickly; he died in less than three months. We battled emotions, had to make critical decisions about his care while running a business.

Most of us eventually will have to deal with the death of our parents. It was especially difficult for me because my dad was just 65 and robbed of his much deserved golden years.

I wished we'd talked about more things – I had so many unanswered questions. In the dozen or so years after his death, I had days in the business when I needed his consul.

Don't take your parents for granted. Their wisdom is priceless and there will come a day when you wish you had spent more time with them.

While Tom **"Defied the Immediate"** in his brief battle with cancer, it took him far too soon. He Defied the Immediate all his life. Everything our family had, he struggled and sacrificed to attain, and he overcame immense obstacles.

Never pass up a chance to talk with your parents; never be too busy to see them. One day they will be gone and the regrets will haunt you. The older you get the greater the blessings of parents are.

Don't ignore the wisdom, experience and love they can provide. Tomorrow may be too late.

CHAPTER 18

Life on the Boards: Who Are We Serving?

"Leadership is not about a title or a designation. It's about impact, influence and inspiration. Impact involves getting results, influence is about spreading the passion you have for your work, and you have to inspire teammates and customers."
— Robin S. Sharma, bestselling author
and leadership expert

Many professionals freely lend their talents as volunteers within their professions and communities. The busiest people are often the best board members because they know how to get things done. They typically are asked to join a particular board for a specific skill set or expertise to help lead an organization.

Apparently, I'm one of those people who organizations seem to call upon when things need to get done. I'm not sure if it's my talent or my inability to say no that has led to my heavy involvement in volunteer work. Likely the latter!

I'd like to think that my background leads me to many of these places. I have a passion to see things done right and efficiently. I've dealt with so many failures and setbacks that when given the opportunity to excel, I take it. Once I latch on to a project or responsibility, I've learned it's far easier to see it through than waffle in mediocrity.

For some reason, every group or organization I've joined tends to elevate me to leadership positions. I'd like to think it's my vision, ideas and perspective, but more than likely it's everyone else's reluctance to assume authority and accountability. Leadership has never come easy. I can lead, but many times no one follows. This is where it becomes frustrating and most people give up. Apathy is a huge problem in nearly every organization I'm part of, and is the reason many groups struggle to attract new members and grow. Good leaders lead; great leaders motivate. I've seen this time and time again.

I became involved with the Michigan Funeral Directors Association at the district level. I went through the chairs and became president of District 3, which is comprised of eight southwest Michigan counties and which represents about 50 funeral homes and directors. I was tasked with running the quarterly district meetings and trying to get members to attend. I soon learned there was a lot of apathy among the members. At one point many years ago, there was much more camaraderie and commitment to the profession and the association. I was always disappointed in turnout for meetings.

I succeeded the district director who sat on the state MFDA board. I was excited and eager to serve my profession.

One of the things that bothered me terribly was the fact my predecessor had so little communication with the district members. Even as district president, I seldom heard from him. One day I was paged at the funeral home and was that told the director was on the phone and wanted to talk to me. I was somewhat excited, perhaps he had some ideas or insight to share, or perhaps he wanted my opinion on a professional issue. Eagerly, I dropped what I was doing to take the call. My excitement changed when I discovered he was making a perfunctory call soliciting a political action committee donation. I agreed to a donation, but when I hung up, I was a little annoyed and determined that if I ever became a director that a PAC solicitation would not be the first or only time my members heard from me. I vowed that communication would be a big part of my efforts should I get to the board.

I joined the state board in the middle of my predecessor's term after he had been forced to resign because he had illegally used proceeds from pre-paid funerals and was facing prosecution. I had to learn the ropes quickly. I thoroughly enjoyed spending a day with colleagues and friends from around the state at board meetings. Many directors were former classmates at Wayne State and good friends. We dove into big issues for the profession and had discussions about legislation that would affect the business – everything from indigent burial funding to continuing education and other professional issues.

One of the important things we accomplished was working with veterans' organizations to create a way to take care of the long-abandoned cremated remains sitting in funeral homes. Funeral homes have many unclaimed boxes of remains on their premises. We worked with the state's American Legion and VFW to screen the ashes and, if any were veterans, the groups would do the research and paperwork and then take them for burial with honors at a National Cemetery. It was a rewarding effort and we finally laid to rest many long forgotten vets.

After I got a feel for how the board functioned, I felt confident to report to the members in my district. I sent an email of what transpired at board meetings, and otherwise worked hard to keep my constituents informed. Soon after, I got a call from the state's executive director telling me I needed to go through him and not communicate directly with the members. He seemed upset. I was puzzled because much of the apathy in the association was due to a lack of communication. Apparently, my communication with members needed screening. A few times I was chastised for communicating too much! While I was generally accurate in what I sent out, I was told that we needed to have "message alignment" in what we communicated to members. After being trusted as a decision maker with U.S. Navy information when I was a public affairs officer, I found it hard to be censored and second-guessed. I had to realize it was not up to me to speak for the association, even though I was a board member. It was a difficult lesson.

I grew as an association director and enjoyed the time I spent with colleagues. I made many contributions, proposed good ideas and worked hard away from the board on issues and research. I was well connected with many legislators and it helped the association on issues we cared about. Although most board meetings were daylong events, I eagerly anticipated them as another opportunity to serve my profession and work with colleagues.

We had annual board retreats, including one on Mackinac Island, which was a thrill. I learned a lot, keeping in mind that I hoped to rise to the executive committee and ultimately to become the president of the association. It was a vision and path that would never be realized.

Eventually my term as director was expiring and I had to groom myself for the responsibility and accountability moving up the leadership ladder. I was the only person on the board qualified and ready. It appeared inevitable.

I interviewed with the nominating committee and thought it went well. I believed I was the obvious choice. Other board members were interested, but none were current with board knowledge, nor had the recent experience I had with all our issues.

At our final meeting of our term at the Amway Grand Plaza Hotel in Grand Rapids, I was invited to breakfast by the executive committee. The previous night we had roasted the outgoing president.

Expecting a welcome aboard meeting, I was soon crushed when they told me they had selected a member who had served on the board nearly five years earlier, someone I didn't know was in the picture. I was furious they selected someone with no relationship with the existing board. No one on the current board knew him, and he was now in line to become our leader. What were they thinking? Was this organizational politics? I didn't say much, but took it in and tried to process what had happened.

That day, I sat through a painful final board meeting and worked hard to keep my mouth shut. I almost walked out when they announced the new recording secretary, the first progressive chair to the presidency. Not one board member had a comment or question about the selection. Nobody asked "Why him?" Or, why wasn't T. R. selected? Nobody said anything. The deafening silence from my colleagues was painful and disheartening.

I felt betrayed! When it was over, I left as soon as I could without talking to anyone for fear I'd say something I'd regret. I was hurt, pissed off and trying hard to process what had happened.

Fortunately, recent MFDA boards have produced leaders from within, as it should be, and the association seems to be improving. But my days serving the profession were over.

I became more involved with Battle Creek service boards where I had a greater impact and that I found more rewarding, particularly the Battle Creek Community Foundation.

I later chaired the foundation's nominating committee and learned how difficult it is to find and select an organization's leadership. It made me more empathic with what happened to me at MFDA. Still, it was too late to reengage with them. I had lost interest.

In hindsight, MFDA's rejection was the best thing that could have happened to me. The funeral business was changing dramatically, and I had lost good associates in my own business. I would have stressed out my remaining staff and my family, and it would have been impossible to run my funeral home and serve the association well. It also helped provide me with clarity on my future in funeral service.

What I thought was a huge personal setback became a great opportunity for self-examination. I faced the reality that funeral service wasn't my first passion and, as my dad had said, "Life is too damn short..." to not do what you love. I always said that being a funeral director was what I did, not who I was.

Shortly after the episode with the MFDA, the national and state associations dwelled on a discussion of whether the funeral business was a "trade" or a "profession." I thought the entire debate was absurd. If we had to question whether we were a profession, we apparently weren't.

For years I argued to ditch the term "funeral industry" because I believed we were a profession, not an industry. We met every requirement for schooling, licensing and regulation as a profession. We were on par with many other professions such as medicine and law. I felt we needed to hold ourselves up as a profession and act and think like professionals. Most of our conventions and meetings were now centering on how to profit from cremation, rather than striving to promote, maintain and elevate the traditional funeral. In many ways, funeral directors were becoming event planners as all some families wanted was a party for the deceased, which many believed they could do on their own. In general, many people stopped relying on us because of an attitude that today, with the Internet, "Anybody can do this!"

Too many funeral directors were taking short cuts, such as not following legal requirements to put cash for pre-paid funerals into trust. We were losing the professional moral high ground as providers of compassionate care and the public exposure of the bad eggs in our profession tainted all of us. It had becoming clear: It was time move on. And I did.

Lesson Learned

Sometimes life hits you between the eyes. I threw my heart and soul into serving my profession on our state board. When I was rejected as a leader, I took it personally and it made me reevaluate my future. While time has passed and I now see the broader scope of what happened, I realized, much like when I was in the Navy, that I was up against a system. The assumptions I made were wrong. I felt that I was the only choice for the association, but factors out of my control dictated another direction.

Things happen for a reason. In this case my rejection led to a series of events that helped create my current life. Had I been selected for the post I sought, it may have destroyed my business and, perhaps, my health. I would have lost my staff and I wouldn't have been successful at either job. It forced me to make a serious examination of my life's mission and goals. In some ways, it was the best thing to happen to me.

I felt I'd been kicked off the team and I took it personally. It's taken me a few years to warm back up to friends and colleagues and to even participate in professional events. Still, I remain a proud member of the Michigan Funeral Directors Association, and will always keep my hard-earned license as a funeral director. I'm proud of all I did, but to continue on would have destroyed me, my business, and my spirit.

I **Defied the Immediate** in what I thought was a terrible injustice, but came out better for having gone through it. Sometimes it takes time and perspective to see all of God's plans. Life is funny that way.

CHAPTER 19

Getting Out While You're on Top

"Risk means everything from being honest about your faith, to moving, to quitting a job that's paying you a fortune but it's not what's in your heart. Risking things is one of the biggest fears we have."

— John Tesh

After my dad died in 2001, my mother, Esther and wife, Kathy worked hard to keep the family enterprise going. I knew it would be a challenge to keep it at the level it was, but I was motivated to prove myself. With my family's help, we not only kept it going, we grew the business.

I dedicated myself to carrying on Dad's legacy by working harder than I ever had. At first it was invigorating and exciting because I took my new role as the business leader so seriously.

I tried to attend as many seminars and business development sessions as I could. Knowledge, I believed, was power. At a marketing session I learned the concept of Face Lots of People, or FLOP. I don't know who came up with the acronym but it resonated with me. The funeral business is personal in the extreme and facing people is the best marketing you can do. For me, that meant engaging with our community, which I loved.

In my Navy career, I excelled at collateral duties, but my main job suffered. Likewise, in the funeral business I probably spent more time doing things outside the business, which I reasoned helped my business. My first love was public relations and it seemed to work for me. The community endeavors were also my de facto social life.

I soon found I needed more help, especially with handling and preparing bodies. We hired another experienced funeral director who enjoyed embalming and preparing bodies for visitations. He had little desire to work on the public side of the business. I was making all the arrangements and helping him out in the prep room when I could and things seemed to be working well. But, unhappy with the expectations I had for him to do all aspects of the business,

The author's wife, Kathy Shaw; the author T.R. Shaw Jr.; the author's mother, Esther M. Shaw, and his sister, Elizabeth Shaw Gescheidle on Sept. 1, 2015 – the final day of the Shaw Funeral Home.

he eventually left for a job in another city for higher pay. In hindsight, his departure was the best thing that could have happened.

For almost a year, I worked harder than ever doing everything, including removals at all hours of the day and night, embalming, and arranging and running funerals while Mom and Kathy deftly managed the office work.

We eventually hired a trade embalmer who did all our body work. I still made most removals and met with families.

Eventually, after a few years of struggling, we hired another experienced funeral director and we became a great team. Our business grew and his wife even came in and worked in the office. We had a successful family business again.

Later, I hired a funeral director who had been a student at Wayne State. I had remembered an impressive paper he had written while at WSU about a military funeral we handled. He had a great work ethic, but he lived in a small town 30 miles from our funeral home. That made it challenging when we had deaths needing immediate attention, and he eventually resigned to work closer to home – a disappointment but not a surprise. I had hoped he'd move to

Battle Creek and help make our business even stronger. Still, I couldn't really blame him.

While things were going well, I was discouraged with the direction and demands of the profession. We had regulatory issues and predatory competitors. Hospice often directed families to homes offering cut-rate (and cut-quality) alternatives. The Fort Custer National Cemetery just west of Battle Creek offered free burials to veterans and the illusion that the entire funeral was free. I got angry almost every time we had a burial there because they had a revolving door of bureaucrats who didn't understand customer service.

The National Cemetery used a government-provided grave liner for nearly all burials. As a result, we lost vault sales. To me, it was about decency and respect. As hard as I tried to convince families that a quality burial vault was preferable to a porous concrete box, I couldn't get people away from the notion that it was free and an entitlement. The grave liners were originally meant to be used if a family had no other means, but it became a benefit. As a veteran myself, I felt strongly that people who served their country deserved better. I would never bury a family member in one of them.

But many people would say, *"It just goes in the ground and nobody sees it."* Well, I saw it and I was typically there until the burial was concluded, unlike many others who took off as soon as possible. That was part of my level of service. I always thought these veterans deserved something better. I also tried to get the government to provide a better vault, but that was like climbing Mount Everest.

Ten years after my dad's death and giving it my all, every day, I was burning out and giving more work to my other funeral directors and staff. We gave my associate funeral director a share of the business and had high hopes that he would eventually take it over. He was an outstanding professional, but I dumped an excessive and unfair workload on him as I became reluctant to engage with families and my passion for the business faded. I was creating a hostile work environment as I slacked off.

He had wanted his own funeral home and I thought of him as the heir apparent, but my behavior, not surprisingly, turned him off. I often was reluctant to even answer the phone because I didn't want to deal with problematic families. People around me knew it was time for me to get out of the business. I occasionally became short with people and said things a leader and professional shouldn't. I wanted to escape. I felt I was still giving families my undivided attention, and for the most part I was. But I couldn't cope with the details required for superior service. I had daily bouts of anxiety and stress because I was running an enterprise that I no longer had passion for.

I felt that funeral directors were no longer viewed as professional service providers and caregivers. I especially grew tired of prospective clients calling and asking: *"What's your cheapest cremation?"* Often, people under duress were price shopping at the time of death.

I engaged a pre-need salesperson to sell contracts for future funerals so I could devote more time to our immediate funerals. It was hard to do both.

Many years ago, we had a retired funeral director who knew funeral service and was adept at working with people on prepaid funerals. But it was very different with the pre-need company we contracted with when I was determined to lighten my workload. They interviewed candidates and we got to select from among them. Still, I had a bad feeling about sending a commissioned salesperson out to do the work of a funeral director. My fears were eventually realized. This person was a highly trained seller of insurance, but not adept in counseling people on funeral service.

Many funeral directors love these programs because they can let the pre-need company put on an aggressive marketing campaign and sign a huge portfolio of future business, while the company makes money selling its insurance plan. The funeral home doesn't have to pay the salesperson and they get the pre-need. The problem came when the sales representative approached families whom we had spent years working with to build excellent relationships. I wasn't comfortable sending someone else out to do a job when people in our community expected to see me.

I felt I was driving away good families by sending someone out with "a bargain in a briefcase" as my friend and funeral director Tom Lynch said. I terminated the program for fear of losing families and went back to a passive pre-need program and took care of people as they sought us out. My theory was that pre-need arrangements were the beginning of an intimate relationship, not a retail experience or sales event. People seek pre-need because they want security, peace of mind and professional advice. Aging and terminal issues can be frustrating and embarrassing for many seniors. They don't know who to trust. Aggressive sales techniques eroded the funeral director's stature and credibility.

The irony of it all was that the business was strong, our reputation in the community was sterling and the business kept growing. But differently. Looking ahead, I didn't see a profitable future or, for that matter, a profession I wanted to continue in. As hard as I tried, I couldn't bring myself to think positively about my future in the funeral business. I went to seminars seeking inspiration, but came back thinking that what I learned wouldn't work in my business or community. I was ready to move on.

Then the funeral director and his wife who were still at the Shaw Funeral Home resigned. I was speechless. I knew I hadn't handled things well with them, not including him in some major decisions and putting far too many burdens on him as I backed off being a professional and leader. I was hurt and disappointed but realized I had only myself to blame.

On the same day our husband-wife team resigned, we had a family discussion and I decided it was time to sell the business. My passion and drive were gone. I still worked hard and took good care of families, but when half my team left, I was ready to lock the door and walk away.

I contacted our financial consultant who works with many funeral homes around the Midwest and told him I wanted to sell and asked if he knew of anyone interested in buying. He reached out to a few who contacted us, but no serious interest developed.

We chatted with a few colleagues, but nobody wanted to make the investment. It was a strong and respected business, but the price was out of the reach for many.

Eventually, the funeral director in nearby Marshall came forward. Craig Kempf had grown a successful family business about 10 miles east of Battle Creek and had the capital and vision to take it over. I was thrilled because he had a young and dynamic staff – some of the people I could never find or get to work for me. He was progressive and throughout our negotiations worked to purchase the adjacent property – something we once considered. His staff jumped in and helped us during the transition. I was thrilled our 106-year-old family business would continue with a strong, passionate funeral director.

During the transition, my sister Elizabeth, who was an officer in our business, was the negotiator. She had done this several times in her business career. She helped our business remain strong and vibrant. I handled families and didn't have to worry about negotiations. I ran funerals right up until the day we signed the papers.

A few days before we signed, as I realized I would be doing my last funeral and driving my last procession, I felt some melancholy. I was always honored to lead a funeral. But I knew it was time to move on.

I miss serving the families we were honored to help through difficult times, but don't miss the drama of dealing with the dysfunctional families we also served. The pressure of unethical competitors in the marketplace, inability to find good help, and a changing attitude toward funeral service would not be missed.

On Sept. 1, 2015, we all got together, signed the papers and transferred what was Battle Creek's first funeral home. We all went out for dinner and drinks, and I began a new and challenging life.

The next day, I took a long drive to South Haven and walked to the end of the pier on Lake Michigan and digested what had happened and where I would go next. A new day was dawning.

But I discovered I wasn't prepared for all the people who asked "How's retirement?" I didn't feel like I had retired. I was only 55. I also equated retirement with laziness, after working nearly every day since I was 15. I resented being associated with those who were no longer contributing members of the workforce. I wasn't ready for that. Instead of retiring, I was organizing my own public relations firm, writing a book, and engaging in community service. Ironically, I had several friends my age who really did retire and they love it and rave about it. It puzzled me.

Needless to say, I was dealing with a new life without income. I was still five years from collecting my Navy pension. I was fortunate to have been a conservative investor and lived frugally. My wife Kathy had taken on an adjunct teaching position at Kellogg Community College and was a partner in my new venture. Money was not the problem, relevance was. I had to learn to embrace the freedom of living life on my schedule. For years I always had someplace to be and something to get done. I had to deal with a new normal.

I had to discipline myself to stay engaged. I eventually responded *"I'm not retired, I'm building my fourth career!"* I would keep myself open for the next big opportunity. Even writing this book took much effort and self-discipline.

Occasionally, I had regrets when a death of someone in our circle of friends was serviced by a competitor's funeral home. At first it bothered me. I got over it. Life goes on.

Lesson Learned

I tried my hardest to push through anxiety and loss of enthusiasm for funeral service. But as the days went on, it became clear I needed to move on while our business was still strong and viable.

If I had stayed in the business, I would never have been completely happy.

A strong leader knows when it's time to leave to make way for new challenges and passions. Eventually the paradigm will shift and you must deal with it or let someone else do it if you can't.

The funeral profession was moving away from my comfort zone into realms I hated. We were geared for service and the new normal was about cost-cutting – service be damned! I **Defied the Immediate** as long as I could. I felt I made a wise personal and financial decision as the world and market was changing. It was difficult leaving something that had been a big part of my life for 30 years and more than a century in our family.

The time had come to muster my confidence and embrace potential risks. I was given an opportunity few people experience. There would be challenging days ahead and times when hindsight would haunt me. But the fears were never realized and new opportunities were there to seize. Life does indeed go on!

CHAPTER 20

Living for yourself

"Give yourself permission to move on!"

– T.D. Jakes

After getting out of the funeral business and being free to pursue my dreams and ambitions, I found it hard to self-motivate. For a long time I wallowed in self-doubt. Did I make a monumental mistake or was it a bold and life-affirming decision?

I've always been one to overthink almost everything. A few months after leaving, I caught an interview with TV star, author and motivator T.D. Jakes.

Sometimes things hit you like a freight train. I had never heard of Bishop T.D. Jakes, a charismatic African-American pastor based in Dallas. He has been named America's best pastor by Time magazine and has been involved in many motivational seminars and films. Jakes has received numerous awards, especially from the black community, but his ministry, motivational messages and reach transcend race.

I came across Jakes during the holiday season on "CBS This Morning," a show I watch daily. At the end of the year, they had many features and commentators on resolutions. His comments struck a chord with me.

He talked about the time we are living in and the "noise" we have to deal with on a daily basis – the noise of technology, media and our infinite capacity to compare ourselves with other people. *"We are destructed by the beauty of other people's lives to the detriment of our own."* He argued that we really need introspection. Most of us don't stop and ponder the beauty and strength that lies in all of us because we are seeing others through the filters of the media.

He talked about changing yourself, and not being afraid of change. *"What gives you fulfillment at one stage of your life might not be what gives you fulfillment at the next stage of your life. Give yourself permission to move on."*

Many people stay trapped in jobs, relationships and commitments that no longer create happiness or inspire others. We must not ignore our sense of destiny.

In his most recent book, "Destiny: Step into your Purpose," he talks a great deal about changing and moving on, something I was dealing with.

This is exactly where I was when we sold the funeral business. For months after the sale, it was hard not look back with some remorse. Self-doubt is a demon many of us face daily. Are we good enough? What could I have done differently?

Jakes made the case that *"We evolve, we go through seasons. You don't fail at something just because the season is over."*

Jakes argues that destiny pulls you away from destruction and that's something we need to heed and pay attention to. It was just what I needed to hear at that time! I think God has a way of bringing things to our attention when we need them most.

Tomorrow Never Waits

It's my opinion that we have an inner voice that never fails us. On so many occasions my experience is that the "gut feeling" we get has always been right.

The problem many of us have is overthinking problems and pretty much everything else. In the military, many of my fitness reports stated that indecision was one of my biggest faults. I learned too late that a good leader makes quick decisions, right or wrong, but also needs to be confident in that decision. Sometimes I made no decision, hoping the situation would change. Sometimes that strategy worked, most of the times it didn't.

The point is, we all have a destiny. Sometimes it is clear, most of the times it is not. We all need to continue to learn from our shortcomings and mistakes. It's the only way we can really move forward.

Steve Jobs said it well in one of his quotes near the end of his life: *"Your time is limited, so don't waste it living someone else's life. Don't be trapped by dogma, which is living with the results of other people's thinking. Don't let the noise of other people's opinions drown out your own inner voice. And most important, have the courage to follow your heart and intuition."*

The Drive to Survive

Leaving the funeral business was hard, very hard. It was such a big part of my family and my life for so many years. Quite frankly, we go through grief when we make a life-changing move, something I've talked about. I've seen people attempt to avoid grief at a time of death, but it can't be done. Grief is something we all have to go through whether it's by a death or a dramatic change in our lives.

I once had a family who simply wanted their mother cremated with no services or any recognition of her life. They were perfunctory about it and even stated, "We just don't do that grief thing." People like this are typically highly educated intellectuals. I was astounded when I heard that. It went against all my training, experience and sensibility. It's times like that you should challenge their belief, but I just had to let it go. The grief will manifest itself eventually, I reasoned.

I still struggle with the premature death of my father and that weighed heavily on my decision to leave funeral service. Grief over his death is still part of my psyche. I wondered what he would do or think about our plans to sell the business. I thought if he were in my shoes, he'd do the same thing.

If someone isn't motivated or excited about what they do, it shows. I was finding myself less and less eager to deal with families and often pawned off dealing with a family to my associates. Although I never slacked off on service or details, the fact I wasn't happy was beginning to show. There was no longer a "fire in the belly" so to speak. I had an attitude I couldn't hide, no matter how hard I worked or put on a game face.

One of the things I once read stated that the mark of a true leader is knowing when to move on. No matter what field you are in, there comes a time when you no longer can do the job to the best of your abilities. It's time to realize that you've reached the limits of your destiny in that place.

Paradigms shift and a new mindset is often needed. A good leader will recognize this and either change with the times or be crushed by it. The old joke about the worker who claimed disability benefits because he was injured when a paradigm shifted has an element of truth to it.

The funeral business was and is changing rapidly and no matter how many good ideas I brought back from seminars, nothing seemed to work very well. Society is drifting away from traditions and religion and it's reflected in how we honor our dead. I admit I was a traditionalist. I believed in the healing powers of ritual and acknowledgment when it came to death. Many faiths still embrace this, but as more and more of us, especially the younger generations, shun traditions, we see a rise in deaths of convenience.

I remember years ago when our funeral home made closed signs for local businesses when they closed shop to attend a funeral. A death brought everyone to a halt and everyone went to the funeral. Typically, there were two days of visitation at the funeral home and a big service within the church or at the funeral home.

Today, the cremation rate is soaring and it's primarily for the convenience of the living. Everyone is just too busy to gather for a funeral. Part of this is our mobile society of course, but most times the overwhelming thought is that we can just do a service for grandma at a more convenient time. Sometimes that never happens.

The other trend I was seeing was the avoidance of grief through "Celebrations of Life." It is a term I absolutely hated to use. It is a synonym for a party, which for many was a way to avoid grief and feeling bad. At a seminar, Rabbi Earl Grollman, one of the leading experts in grief and dying, alluded to the fact that grief avoidance is the root of many societal problems today. He said grief cannot be avoided; everyone must go through it at some point in their life.

Many of these celebratory events leave people emotionally empty and struggling with grief. Someone once asked me, *"Why do they call them celebrations when it's so sad?"* I really couldn't answer that. One widow I served who just had a "party" at the country club, because that's what her husband wanted, said to me, *"The only thing I got out of that was a bar bill."*

For many of us, the funeral profession is a calling. However, I never felt that way. It was what I did, not who I was. Although I believe I was an extremely good funeral director and always was a consummate professional in both business and social life. I played the role well, but my inner voice was telling me something different.

I saw things changing around me, most of which I couldn't control. I saw many in the profession trying hard to capitalize on cremation to the detriment of traditional funeral service. Nearly every professional seminar I attended focused on how to "Profit from Cremation." I don't ever recall a session on "Preserving the Traditional Funeral." In many communities, competing firms were racing to bankruptcy by undercutting each other to provide cheaper services.

When someone would inquire about our "cheapest" cremation (the FTC requires price disclosures; cremation was 99% of our price inquiries), I said I don't have any cheap services, we are a full-service funeral home, here are my prices, which are reasonable, and this is what we offer. I didn't win over many who were shopping solely on price, but then again I wasn't Wal-Mart. I felt vindicated that I was protecting the value of funeral service by not lowering standards to compete. Frankly, the cheap providers aren't providing much of a service and most families will never use them more than once because they had expected more. I believe that many of the rock-bottom providers are simply unethical if not immoral in how they handle human dispositions.

I also was seeing the hospice movement, which has been a great thing in terminal care, overstep their bounds and refer families to the cheapest providers for funeral service. There was little I could do about it. I could never understand how, after providing such loving and compassionate care, hospice workers could turn families over to these providers. Some hospices offer a death bed visitation and celebration before they contact us to help a family circumvent the cost of a funeral.

Additionally, many "progressive" churches are usurping the duties of funeral directors by offering celebrations, telling families they will take care of the services, suggesting they just do a simple cremation and don't waste their money. (Give it to us instead!) I've attended a few "celebrations" with no body and no funeral director present. They were not good services. It's terribly unfair to church volunteers to have to figure out how to accommodate people and "direct" a funeral. I was always grateful to pastors who understood our role and adamantly refused to do any funeral or memorial service without a funeral director present. They are few and far between today.

With the lack of traditional burials, casket salesmen were offering the very bottom of their product lines. Many times we also competed with the VA as many viewed a graveside service at the National Cemetery as a free funeral. The problem is that the VA only schedules 30-minute intervals that are meant to be strictly committal in nature. When families expected a full service at the grave they felt cheated and angry because they got pushed out by the next burial coming in. When people expressed that everything's free at the VA, I reminded them that no, it's at taxpayer expense and you have to live by the agency's excessive rules and regulations.

While well intended, those services typically do not help the family cope with grief and loss. It was frustrating having to deal with these issues.

All this was gnawing on me and as hard as I tried, there was little I could do about them. Beyond the funeral issues, our associations were constantly dealing with cumbersome and overzealous state and federal business regulations. I was always frustrated that while Michigan had a high trusting standard for pre-need funding, other states did not. I expressed the need to our national association for a singular pre-need standard in the nation. I saw many families get taken in other states by hustlers and charlatans claiming to be funeral directors.

As hard as I tried, I could not accept and work with these new paradigms. The funeral business was no longer the profession I began in or aspired to. I got sick of hearing about "adapting to change," but I could not adapt to change I didn't believe in. Most of it was change for change sake. Frankly, funeral service is reactive instead of proactive. Funeral service moved toward minimization and cremation because that's what we collectively believed people wanted. I still believed people wanted closure, honesty, value and tradition when taking care of the dead.

Economics was rarely a factor in determining disposition. In fact, nearly all of the minimal services I provided were to people of wealth. A psychologist once told me that people of wealth exercise a great deal of control throughout their lives in a number of things. Death is one thing out of their control and they deal with it by not dealing with it.

The traditional funeral is becoming a thing of the past. I grew tired of taking bodies to the crematory and often felt I was the only one who cared. The sooner I could move on, the better. My heart was no longer there.

Every Successful Person in This World Has Jumped

Steve Harvey is a gifted television personality. A while back he made headlines and was the butt of many jokes for a monumental mistake of announcing the wrong winner of the Miss Universe pageant. It was embarrassing and humiliating for the true winner and Harvey, and it had to be corrected on the spot. But Harvey didn't blame officials or others around him. He took full responsibility for the gaff even if it wasn't really his actual mistake.

One day in my Facebook feed someone shared a brief talk he did with his audience following the taping of "Family Feud," which he hosts.

In his impromptu chat with the audience, he talked about "jumping." That was later the title of his best-selling book "Jump."

He started by saying, "Let me tell you this; every successful person who has ever lived has jumped!" He went on to explain what he was talking about. He stated that too many people are stuck in their positions in life, be it work at a job they hate, bad relationships, etc. "God, when he created all of us, gave us a gift at birth. If we are not using that gift, whatever it may be, we need to jump." He equated it with standing on a cliff and watching others flying by because they are using their gifts and talents. "When you are standing on the cliff of life seeing everyone flying by, they are living in their gift. The only way for you to soar is to jump off that cliff. It's the only way to see what real living is like. If you don't jump, your parachute will never open."

He then said, "I'm not going to kid you. Many times that parachute will not open fully and you will be trashed on the rocks. You will be bloody and hurt, but God will eventually open the parachute. You can play it safe and stay where you are, but God's gift will never be realized, because that chute will never be opened. My advice to you is to make the decision to jump."

Harvey's philosophy struck a chord with me. His impromptu speech and later his book confirmed that leaving the funeral business was the right thing to do.

In his book he opens up about the difficulties and challenges of his life before fame and fortune. It's a must-read for anyone stuck in a bad situation.

I had already jumped when I heard this and devoured his book when it came out. Harvey inspired me to keep moving forward. His timing in my life couldn't have been better. All of us have to jump at some point. It's not easy, but it must be done to live fully and I just did it!

Lesson Learned

Mustering courage never comes easy for anyone. We all must realize that we have a destiny we must heed. Most of us never realize or understand our true destiny because we are trapped in a bad or economically driven situation.

Most people might dream of chasing after a dream job or eventually doing what they always wanted to do, but that weekly paycheck is standing in the way. Many will stay in jobs they hate and tolerate horrible working conditions because it provides a good income. These are jobs that provide a living, but not a life.

Many don't have the courage to "jump" as Steve Harvey has said. Jumping is hard; it takes a great deal of faith and courage to truly pursue your dreams and passions.

I had to overcome many fears when I "jumped" from funeral service. I gave up a 106-year-old family institution. I feared community and professional reaction and backlash, but none of those fears came to pass. I **Defied the Immediate,** which ended up being a phantom.

Actually, I felt a great sense of pride and personal satisfaction knowing I "jumped" at the right time as the profession was changing and moving away from my professional comfort zone. I felt liberated from what was holding me back from pursing my true passion, which is writing and public affairs work. I was fortunate that I sold a business at the top of its game and did not have to abandon a sinking ship. I realized I had a great support system around me with family and friends who were there for me when I needed a sounding board.

Don't let the opinions of others hold you back from realizing your destiny. Your fears often never materialize and your gut feeling is usually right. Heed it and live for yourself, not others.

CHAPTER 21

Life is Short; Live Your Passion

"Learn to enjoy every minute of your life. Be happy now. Don't wait for something outside of yourself to make you happy in the future. Think how really precious is the time you have to spend, whether it's at work or with your family. Every minute should be enjoyed and savored."

— Earl Nightingale

"You'll have a dog for only part of your life; the dog will have you for his entire life."

— A Facebook post

I once had a wonderful dog, a purebred chocolate Lab I got from a friend who breeds dogs and knows the best ones. The dog was with me through some of my best years.

My energetic puppy was a handful. I named her Zap because I had heard dogs need a short simple name. It helps when you call them. I specifically chose the name Zap because "American Gladiators," a popular television show at the time, featured Zap, a strong and admirable female gladiator. Contestants on the show ran an obstacle course lined with the gladiators, California bodybuilders in revealing spandex outfits who blocked their way. The gladiators had names like Turbo, Blaze, Ice and Zap.

Yes, it was cheesy, but I was young and single. A little embarrassed about my real reason, I invented a different story to explain Zap's name. I told people her puppy diet was extension cords and TV remotes. That part was true! I had to buy at least two new remotes before I broke her of that habit.

Anyway, Zap was a free spirit. She couldn't sit still – a real issue for a hunting retriever. And Zap loved everyone. She would follow joggers home and I'd have to retrieve her when they called the phone number on her collar. She loved going to our cottage on Gull Lake, racing to the water as soon as we'd arrive. I had a rubber bumper, a device used to train retrieving dogs. I'd heave it out into the lake and she'd run down the dock, make a leap, and retrieve it, over and over.

In the evening, she would walk into the living room and collapse from exhaustion. She slept well.

She also loved the boat and we couldn't pull away from the dock unless she was in the house. One time we left her behind and she attempted to swim out to us. She'd bark and whine if she saw us leave. When she was in the boat, she'd race to the bow with her nose into the wind.

She often would jump out of the boat to chase ducks. Getting her back in the boat was always a challenge.

Although Zap gave us joy and good times, her life was brief. She lived six human years, about 40 dog years. One day she started moping around and wasn't eating. We took her to the vet and got the bad news. She had an inoperable liver tumor that got worse a few weeks later. This came at the same time my dad was going through chemo and was in his final days. I don't know what kind of pain she suffered, but she knew I was in pain for my dad.

Dad died in January 2001 and, within a month, I faced the inevitable and euthanized my best friend. I was racked with grief and emotions and held off making the decision for a long time. One day, she became very ill, and couldn't eat anything and I had to schedule the appointment. It was one of the most emotional days of my life. The drive to the vet was painful. Kathy sat in back of the station wagon with Zap. I knew I was making the right decision, but it just didn't feel right considering the unconditional love she had given us.

It took me days to stop sobbing when I thought about her. I still do on occasion. While some put on a strong face, no one can avoid grief and it never goes away – with humans or pets. I've seen people try to avoid it, but they can't.

2001 was one of the worst years of our lives. In January I lost my dad and in February we had to put Zap down. Kathy lost her father Arthur Banfield in May. We lost Aunt Peg, my grandfather's only sister, in November.

Then Sept. 11, 2001, came and, in an instant, changed the world forever. Could things get worse?

On New Year's Eve 2002, we said good riddance to our 2001 calendars, tossing them in the fireplace.

No year since has been so difficult. It is written that sometimes we must "Walk through the Valley of the Shadow of Death." 2001 was that walk for our family.

As a funeral director, I've embalmed and prepared the bodies of many people, young and old. I've stood over the embalming table of many 50-somethings, mostly cancer victims. It was disturbing to see so many people my age.

It forced me to think about where I was going with my life. The saying – "Therefore but by the Grace of God, go I" – rang in my head.

I've also tended to many people who died in what should have been the prime of their life; people who were alcoholics as well as young people felled by terrible diseases, accidents or at their own hands in suicide.

Some of the deaths made me very sad, others made me angry. My close association with death gave me a greater appreciation of life.

Fortunately, I've also processed many who lived long, happy and healthy lives well into their 90s. It's a different grief but, philosophically, their longevity has connected them with many people. Can you imagine how many people a 100-year-old man or woman has touched with their life?

106-year-old Danny Olmstead of Bellevue may have been the oldest person we had the honor to provide a funeral for. He had 11 children and, at his death, 165 living descendants. For his 100th birthday Bellevue's Main Street was closed down for a party. Asked his secret to longevity, he replied, "Well, I never smoked, I never drank and I never chased women…'til I was 14!" A good sense of humor undoubtedly aided his longevity.

The elderly have a huge circle of family and friends who know them. While it's sad to see them depart, it is inevitable and accepted. There is still grief.

My dad died at age 65 in a quick battle with lymphoma. It took him down in less than three months. He was cheated out of his Golden Years.

His father, Frank Jr., died in 1966 of colon cancer at 56 and his grandfather, Frank Sr., left us at 52. Unfortunately, in the 1960s we didn't have the detection and treatment options we have today. Had my dad or Frank Jr. lived another 20 years, medical advances might have saved them. The fact that longevity doesn't seem to be genetically on my side weighed heavily on my decision to give up funeral service.

Even before dad was diagnosed, it seemed he had premonitions about his fate. He had begun easing out of the funeral business and made comments like "our time on this good Earth is just too short," which became almost self-fulfilling.

Like me, he had seen death in the young and the old, and knew that our time here is finite, and that life is a precious gift. We need to do something with it while we can, the best that we can.

As I reached middle age, I looked back on all the people I looked up to when I was growing up. When we were children, there were a lot of elderly people in our lives who are now gone. Consider grandparents or possibly great-grandparents who we scarcely remember. Our time with them was brief in the span of our lifetime. Like the life of a dog, they are only with us for part of our lives.

My thoughts on the brevity and unpredictability of life make it imperative

The author at a military storytelling event recounting his awkward fascination with several hundred dolphins while standing watch on an aircraft carrier – much to the delight of the audience, and dismay of the ship's top officers.
(Photo by Al Lassen, Battle Creek ENQUIRER)

that we live our dreams, face our fears and maximize the present. Tomorrow is promised to no one. I've seen death claim rich, poor, young and old. I've seen far too many lost opportunities because someone was foolish with their choices. It sometimes angers me, but that anger has given me this book as a platform to try to help people realize that all we have is the here and now.

Motivational speaker Orrin Woodward once asked an audience if they were dreaming of reaching the mountaintop or living at the base camp? Far too many people never leave the comfort and security of the base camp. They may dream about getting to the mountaintop. They may even see it, but too few do it. Why?

I also understand that the fear of success is almost as stifling as the fear of failure. For many, failure is a comfortable and familiar place. Success takes effort, courage and, most important, a willingness to take risks! It means getting out of your comfort zone and having the courage to live your dreams. It takes getting knocked down and getting back up. Over and over and over.

I believe people are engineered for greatness and we are the only ones holding ourselves back. The problem is that too many of us simply make bad choices in life and never connect with those who can help us. Most of us never learn what it takes to succeed. Most of us are stuck in the base camp.

Dr. Denis Waitley was a Naval Academy graduate, Vietnam pilot and a Navy public affairs colleague. He later became a psychologist and mental skills coach for Olympic athletes. He wrote in his book, "The Winners Edge," that winning and success is about working smarter, not harder! Most of us just haven't been motivated to seek the best advice for success in our lives.

Resources and people can help get you there. It's easy if you try! Most people don't and make excuses. Don't be one of them.

The superstars in life haven't gotten there by accident or luck. They failed until they found success. I've failed more often than I want to admit. Sometimes it was so devastating and embarrassing that I didn't think I could keep going. But I did. I defied the immediate!

Looking back, most of my failures were huge learning experiences that I had to go through, much like grief – to get ahead. You never know how close you are to success, in anything, until you take the next step. Sometimes, many more steps.

Achieving success is not the end of the challenge. It takes maintenance and knowledge to stay on top because the world changes.

Students entering college today, embarking on a career in almost anything, may have an obsolete knowledge base by the time they graduate. If the student doesn't accept and embrace that learning must be continual, he will fall behind quickly.

Sometimes the answers are found in books, reading that too few of us are doing in today's electronic world.

The local bookstore when I was growing up in Battle Creek, had a slogan under their sign that read:"READERS ARE LEADERS!" It's true!

The Rich Lessons of Failure

Billionaire and philanthropist Bill Gates said, "It's fine to celebrate success but it is more important to heed the lessons of failure."

Never fear failure or success.

Failure is the incubator of character. Don't let fear of failure prevent you from trying anything.

Nobody is perfect out of the gate. We forget that Michael Jordan missed more than half his shots during his NBA career, yet he's hailed as perhaps the greatest of all time. Major League Baseball pays big bucks to a .300 hitter. That means that 7 out of 10 times at bat he makes an out, yet he's considered an elite hitter.

On the flip side, would you want your surgeon or accountant to be a .300 hitter?

Success is incremental and time-consuming and getting there requires knowledge and experience and discovering what doesn't work. Thomas Edison failed hundreds of times before perfecting the incandescent light bulb. Failures often teach us more about success than does success. Edison said he never failed, he just found hundreds of ways it didn't work!

If you want success, you must keep "Defying the Immediate."

It's Your Choice

So what are you doing with the time you have left? Are you learning about and reaching for goals you once dreamed about? If not, what's stopping you?

Have you accepted that you are unlucky, doomed and unworthy of hanging with the Big Dogs?

The people you admire and aspire to be like have been in your position. They made many mistakes and failures to reach where they are today.

I'm here to tell you, as someone who has seen death in its many forms, when it's over it's over. None of us get out of this life alive. We have to maximize the time we have here to do those things that improve ourselves and improve society.

Too many of us underestimate the immense freedom that comes with being healthy and vibrant. Freedom to succeed or fail! We don't realize what we can do until we can't do it any longer. If you can get up in the morning, if you can read, if you can imagine, then you have what it takes. The rest is just details.

Too many of us squander our potential with a bad attitude or hanging with the wrong people. Run from those who would pull you down. Fly with the eagles!

Reach out to those who can help you succeed. I've found that most successful people want to be asked for help. In general, very successful people, in almost any field, are humble, grateful and eager to share their wisdom. They are usually honored to be asked for their advice.

I stumbled for years trying to figure things out on my own. We live in a connected society and people can and will help you.

Someday you'll be the one being asked for help. Return the favor! In "The Winner's Edge," Waitley wrote: "The real winners in life get what they want by helping others get what they want. Independence has been replaced by inter-dependence. There are too many people, too few resources and too delicate a balance between nature and technology to produce winners in isolation today."

Someday, you may be looked up to and admired. Success is not a selfish act. Reciprocity is a mark of greatness.

That's what true leaders do.

That's what great people do.

+++

It's always appropriate to end a sermon, which I feel this book is, with a prayer. I kept this from a service I attended with my sister's family in Lake Forest, Illinois. It gives me great comfort and I return to it often:

Prayer of Confession Lake Forest Presbyterian Church, Sept. 23, 2012

Gracious God, as you once breathed life into the Earth at its birth, breathe your Spirit into us now.

We confess that we are tired of trying to be everything to everyone;

Of seeking the World's approval and conforming to the culture's image of what we should be.

Refresh us with your image of our lives.

We confess that we are embarrassed by our pride and perfectionism, by our failure of nerve and by our selfish preoccupations.

Reclaim us with your cleansing love.

We confess that we are confused by all the expectations we encounter, by competing demands on our time and by our own heart's desires.

Revive us with your clarity of purpose.

Amen.

Final thoughts: Choose to be a leader. Choose to be great. Share your journey. Keep moving forward and ... Defy the Immediate!

Godspeed!

EPILOGUE

Final Lesson Learned...
Why We Need to Live in the Present

"Your work is going to fill a large part of your life, and the only way to be truly satisfied is to do what you believe is great work. And the only way to do great work is to love what you do. If you haven't found it yet, keep looking. Don't settle. As with all matters of the heart, you'll know when you find it."

— Steve Jobs

A great philosopher once said that if you dwell in the past and think too much about the future, you will miss the present. He was right. Now is the only time we have.

My years in the military and the funeral profession taught me about the brevity of life. Over the years I saw terrible, tragic deaths. I saw too much unfulfilled potential. I saw lives wasted in substance abuse and poor lifestyle choices. I saw lives cut short by cancer, chronic disease and unfortunate accidents.

I believe none of us are here on this Earth by accident. We are the products of millions of years of evolution and are masters of our destiny. We have brains that can be shaped by knowledge and experience, so be careful how you grow it and who you surround yourself with. How we deal with external circumstances defines us.

In the first chapter I discussed reconnecting with your inner child. The child who dreamed big dreams with no understanding of limitations. Stop and think that those grandiose dreams were likely snuffed out by negativity and opinions of those around us. Too many times as we grew up we listened to the wrong voices and muted our inner child.

With our brains, we can evaluate the experiences and results of those who have already forged a path. We can learn from others and continue to constantly evaluate the path ahead in our lives. We don't have to believe everything we see

171

or hear. There are many people and voices in this world we should ignore. It's up to us to decide who we listen to.

Part of reality is criticism from others. Too many of us pay far too much attention to what others might think or say about us, and it keeps us from moving forward. Aristotle once said that there are only three ways to avoid criticism: Do Nothing, Say Nothing and Be Nothing. Likewise, we must not let compliments get to our head, nor criticism get to our hearts.

When I sold our funeral home, I feared the opinions of others. I feared I was letting a lot of people down. I felt I might get branded a fool for not sticking with it. I feared I was turning my back on a worthy profession. I feared I was letting down my deceased father, who along with my mother loved the business. I was wrong; most people understood and knew the challenges I was facing. Most everyone was grateful for the services we provided and wished me well. Some were inspired that I made such a courageous and difficult decision. Life goes on.

The truth is we have to do what's in our own best interest and not listen to the biased opinions of others. We need to listen to the voices of wisdom and reason and make an educated decision based on our passion and beliefs.

When we live in the present, we see the beauty of the moment and can capture the truths of our world. We can learn to distinguish the good from the bad and take forward only the best on our journey. If we drag the baggage of the past or look too far forward, we miss the golden nuggets at our feet that will guide us forward.

As a society, we're wrapped up in technology and things that separate us as humans. Far too many of us are engrossed in social media, which is robbing us of intimate personal relationships. Social media and being connected is import-ant to a point. I've spent a lot of time on social media "building my platform." But when we live in virtual reality, we are missing out on life's great moments.

Our invasive 24/7 news media dwells on the negative and absurd and doesn't truly reflect reality. We are living in a time when the world's greatest communication system is at our fingertips, yet we aren't really communicating on a personal level. Automation and technology in many ways is destroying us. Maybe this is why we are seeing so much depression, violence and bullying in our world; we've lost the ability to connect on a personal level. Defy it!

Life is a series of moments. Each day we have 86,400 seconds to use for good or nil. It's up to us to make the most of them. As I've seen in the funeral profession, tomorrow is promised to no one.

Get out and live life ... today! Make a difference and Defy the Immediate!

ABOUT THE AUTHOR

Thomas Rocklin (T.R.) Shaw Jr.

Rocklin was the first name of my great-great-grandfather, the first of our branch of the Shaw clan to settle in the Midwest. The family believes he moved from New York after emigrating from Scotland. Our family was not creative with names, so we have lots of juniors and even a few IIIs and IVs in the family tree. Because my dad had the same name first, I've always been known as T.R., except in high school when I was too shy to explain it and just accepted Tom. My mother's side of the family called me Tommy, which I hated, when I was a youngster.

June 7, 1960: Born in Battle Creek.

1964: Sister Elizabeth born.

1974: Began working in student media at W.K. Kellogg Junior High.

1977: Attended Kellogg Community College as an advanced standing student.

1978: Graduated from Battle Creek Central High School.

1978: Enrolled at Central Michigan University and began working at CM LIFE, the student newspaper.

Summer 1979: Completed Outward Bound program in Colorado.

Fall 1979: Pledged Sigma Chi fraternity, Zeta Rho chapter, and later became Chapter Editor and Alumni Relations Officer.

1982: Graduated from Central Michigan University with BAA in journalism.

Fall 1982: Began U.S. Navy Officer Candidate School, Newport, Rhode Island.

Spring 1983: Commissioned ensign in the U.S. Navy and began Surface Warfare Officer School Basic in Newport.

Fall 1983: Reported to USS Dwight D. Eisenhower (CVN 69) on Bagel Station, eastern Mediterranean.

1987: Released from active duty, then began service in U.S. Navy Reserve in Battle Creek.

1987-1999: Served in SEABEE Unit, Destroyer Squadron Unit, NATO Staff Unit.

1989: Graduated with certificate in mortuary science from Wayne State University.

1989: Began career as funeral director with Shaw Funeral Homes, continued in Navy Reserve.

1999: Designated Navy Public Affairs Officer, assigned to Navy Information Bureau, Det. 613, Great Lakes, Illinois.

June 2000: Married Kathy Banfield.

January 2001: Father, Thomas R. Shaw, 65, died four months after diagnosis of non-Hodgkin's lymphoma.

2001: Became president of Shaw Funeral Homes and served on board of Michigan Funeral Directors Association.

2003: Returned to Battle Creek Navy Reserve Center with NATO Unit.

2003: Participated as Public Affairs Officer at commissioning ceremony USS Ronald Reagan (CVN 76).

October 2005: Retired from U.S. Navy Reserve.

September 2015: Sold Shaw Funeral Homes to Kempf Family Funerals Homes of Marshall.

2015: With wife, Kathy, founded Shaw Communication in Battle Creek.

To learn more about the author and to contact him for speaking engagements visit his website: www.trshawjr.com.

Dick Enberg

Dick Enberg is an Armada, Michigan, native, a legendary sportscaster and 1957 graduate of Central Michigan University. Over his more than half-century career, he was a profesional play-by-play announcer for baseball, basketball, football, tennis and the Olympics. He broadcast nine Rose Bowl games and dozens of NCAA Final Fours and Wimbledon tennis tournaments. His broadcasting, writing and production work was honored with 13 Emmy Awards and a Lifetime Achievement Emmy. He even has a star on the Hollywood Walk of Fame. At CMU, he is the namesake for the Dick Enberg Academic Center for Excellence and the annual Dick Enberg Award for Athletic and Academic Achievement. At CMU, he graduated *summa cum laude* in 1957 and was the student body president. Enberg also has a master's degree and a doctorate degree from Indiana University and is the author of his autobiography, "DICK ENBERG, Oh My!" He died suddenly on Dec. 22, 2017. (Special thanks to fellow CMU grad Todd Anson for connecting T.R. Shaw with Enberg.)

ACKNOWLEDGEMENTS

——

Writing is a team effort. Nobody in journalism or the media produces quality work on their own. All great writers have a team of editors, proofers, sounding boards, and yes critics.

I'm grateful for the connections who helped me along the way. In college I had great professors who took the time to care and believe in me. In the military I served under great leaders who inspired me and guided me and gave me opportunities to excel. In business I had colleagues and allies who were always there for me.

When I began the goal of writing a book, I sought the advice of many published authors who are family and friends. Some of those who helped and guided me with their writing experiences were cousin John Shaw, niece Kim Woodard Osterholzer, and good friend and fellow Rotarian, Carlos Fontana.

I'm especially grateful to John Wemlinger, a friend, fellow veteran and accomplished author, who referred me to Mission Point Press and answered many questions along the way. He inspired me with his passion for writing great stories with an even greater purpose behind them.

I'm grateful to the entire team at Mission Point Press for their hard work, guidance and especially patience. Doug Weaver, Bob and Ruth Campbell, Bob Deck and Noah Shaw, along with all the others behind the scenes who make it happen for first-time authors. Dena Phaff Haas, friend and photographer, shot the outstanding cover photo.

Todd Anson, CMU alumnus and now Trustee, was key in connecting me with Dick Enberg. I regret that Enberg didn't live to see the finished product, I think he would have been pleased and excited, especially with the CMU stories. Oh My! He loved CMU.

My sister Liz and mother Esther were right there too during the entire journey with ideas and inspirations. Finally, of course, my wife, proof-reader and chief critic, Kathy Shaw played a huge role in keeping me going, and being my biggest advocate. Thanks for believing in me.

I couldn't have done this without all of these people and many others too countless to name. Thank you to all.

Made in the USA
Columbia, SC
31 December 2019

86030049R00109